*Rebellion,
Revolution,
And Religiousness*

www.OSHO.com

OSHO

A comprehensive multi-language website including a magazine, OSHO Books, OSHO TALKS in audio and video formats, the OSHO Library text archive in English and Hindi and extensive information about OSHO Meditations. You will also frind the program schedule of the OSHO Multiversity and information about the OSHO International Meditation Resort.

To contact **OSHO International Foundation** go to:
www.osho.com/oshointernational

About the Author

Osho's teachings defy categorization, covering everything from the individual quest for meaning to the most urgent social and political issues facing society today. His books are not written but are transcribed from audio and video recordings of extemporaneous talks given to international audiences over a period of 35 years. Osho has been described by the Sunday Times in London as one of the "1000 Makers of the 20th Century" and by American Author Tom Robbins as "the most dangerous man since Jesus Christ."

About his own work Osho has said that he is helping to create the conditions for the birth of a new kind of human being. He has often characterized this new human being as "Zorba the Buddha" -- capable both of enjoying the earthy pleasures of Zorba the Greek and the silent serenity of a Gautam Buddha. Running like a thread through all aspects of Osho's work is a vision that encompasses both the timeless wisdom of the East and the highest potential of Western science and technology.

Osho is also known for his revolutionary contribution to the science of inner transformation, with an approach to meditation that acknow-ledges the accelerated pace of contemporary life. His unique "Active Meditations" are designed to first release the accumulated stresses of body and mind, so that it is easier to experience the thought-free and relaxed state of meditation.

Two autobiographical works by the author are available:
Autobiography of a Spiritually Incorrect Mystic
Glimpses of a Golden Childhood

Rebellion, Revolution, And Religiousness

Osho

NEW FALCON PUBLICATIONS
LAS VEGAS, NEVADA, U.S.A.

Rebellion, Revolution and Religiousness
OSHO

Copyright © 1990, 2010 OSHO International Foundation, Switzerland. www.osho.com/copyrights
All rights reserved.

Osho Image: Copyright © OSHO International Foundation

Original English Title: Rebellion, Revolution and Religiousness

ISBN-10 1561841919
ISBN-13 9781561841912

OSHO is a registered trademark of Osho International Foundation. For further information please go to osho.com/trademark.

The material in this book is selected from various talks by Osho given to a live audience. All of Osho's talks have been published in full as books, and are also available as original audio recordings. Audio recordings and the complete text archive can be found via the online OSHO Library at www.osho.com

NEW FALCON PUBLICATIONS
9550 South Eastern Avenue • Suite 253
Las Vegas, NV 89123
www.newfalcon.com
email: info@newfalcon.com

Preface

The first fundamental is to be a rebel.

All the religions destroy the potential of rebellion in man. Obviously – because to teach rebellion means to teach these people to rebel against tradition, against convention, against society, against religion; and these are their vested interests. Rebellion has to be absolutely slaughtered. But the moment the spirit of rebellion dies in a man, man lives only a posthumous existence – because the spirit of rebellion is your real spirit.

All the religions have taught just the opposite.

They teach you to believe.

I teach you to doubt.

They teach you to have faith.

I teach you to inquire.

They give you everything ready-made. And I am telling you that unless you attain it by your own effort it is absolutely useless. A God that is handed over to you is worth nothing.

A holy scripture that comes through tradition…to simply imbibe it like a parrot is suicidal. You are poisoning yourself because the more knowledgeable you become, the less is the possibility for you to seek, search and find.

Once you get this stupid idea that you know already, the question of inquiry does not arise. The question of inquiry arises only when you feel that you know nothing.

But no religion lets you know that you know nothing. They go on forcing knowledge, catechisms, doctrines, dogmas on you. They are stuffing your mind with all kinds of empty words. A word is always empty unless it contains your experience.

My word cannot be a real nourishment to you. It will be empty – it is only the container. The content? – there is no way to convey the content. I can pass you the container, the word, but how can I pass you my experience which is always left behind? The word goes to you and I see an empty, dead word in your hand. And the thing that I wanted to express, to convey, to transfer, is left behind; it never leaves my being.

Hence, truth is inexpressible.

Only idiots go on talking about truth.

And those idiots believe that what they are saying is true. They are only saying yakketty-yakketty-yak, and nothing else. They are chatterboxes, but they can believe that they are transferring something to you because they themselves don't have anything other than the word. So they feel that they have transferred something.

But a man who knows can never feel that it is possible to transfer truth. Yes, he can inspire you to inquire, but he cannot transfer to you the truth itself.

So the first thing is the spirit of rebellion – which implies doubt, skepticism, inquiry. It needs tremendous courage because you will be going against all, all those who are in power. The politicians, the priests, the super-rich, the pedagogues in the universities – they are all in powerful positions.

Your effort to inquire is a declaration against all of them, because they are saying, "Truth has been found by Jesus Christ; you need not worry about it. You simply believe in Jesus Christ."

Now this is as stupid as somebody saying, "The theory of relativity has been discovered by Albert Einstein. You need not worry about the theory of relativity – simply have faith in Albert Einstein and everything is okay." Do you think by having faith in Albert Einstein you will understand anything about the theory of relativity? What does your faith in Einstein have to do with the theory of relativity? They are not related at all to each other.

The same is the case with Jesus, Krishna, Zarathustra, Buddha, Mohammed. It is not possible for you to know what Jesus knows, just by having faith in Jesus. In the first place, how do you know that he knows? In the second place, how can you destroy the skepticism which is born in you from your very birth?

Faith is being taught.

Doubt is your natural capacity.

Existence gives you the quality of doubt and the vested interests destroy that quality and cover it with beliefs. Beliefs are in their favor, not in your favor.

I am a little bit crazy because I am speaking against my own profession, but I can't help it. I could have become a world teacher with millions of followers if I had not been crazy enough to start telling you the truth. The truth is, all the vested interests are against you: your individuality, your nature, your potentiality.

Osho

Contents

The Art of Freedom	1
Reform, Revolution and Rebellion: The Three Rs of Man's Evolution	9
Priests and Politicians—Parasites in Power	21
Christianity and Communism: Partners in the Same Racket to Exploit the Poor	35
Dictatorship in the Power in Their Hands	49
Freedom Is Not License	55
Consciousness Evolving Means Society Dissolving	59
Terrorism – Your Inner Volcano of Violence	81
The Basic Fallacy of Revolutions	89
Meditation Brings Utopia to Earth	99
Rest in Peace – or in Pieces	121
The Mystery of "Yes"	135
Gnosticism – the Roots of Religious Rebellion	155
The Only Hope Left – Our Will to Live	173
Anarchism and Consciousness	187
Compromise is your Dignity on the Gallows	191
Religiousness and Rebelliousness: Two Names for the Same Phenomenon	201
Meditation is the Only Unselfish Act	209
One Seed Can Make the Whole Earth Green	219
I Belong to Eternity–You Can, Too	225

One

The Art of Freedom

Osho,

Whenever I think about freedom, I'm either trying to escape from something I don't like, or yearning for something I don't have. Would you please talk about the wider implications of freedom?

Freedom *from* is ordinary, mundane. Man has always tried to be free from things. It is not creative; it is the negative aspect of freedom. Freedom *for* is creativity. You have a certain vision that you would like to materialize and you want freedom for it.

Freedom *from* is always from the past, and freedom *for* is always for the future.

Freedom for is a spiritual dimension, because you are moving into the unknown and perhaps, one day, into the unknowable. It will give you wings. Freedom from, at the most, can take away your handcuffs. It is not necessarily beneficial—and the whole of history is a proof of it. People have never thought of the second freedom that I am insisting on; they have only thought of the first, because they don't have the insight to see the second. The first is visible: chains on their feet, handcuffs on their hands. They want to be free from them, but then what? What are you going to do with your hands? You may even repent that you asked for freedom from.

It happened in the Bastille in the French Revolution; it was the most famous French prison, it was reserved only for those who were sentenced to live in jail for their whole lives. So one entered the Bastille alive but never came out alive—only the dead bodies came out. And when they put on the handcuffs, the chains, they locked them and threw the keys, because they were not needed. Those locks would not be opened again, so what would be their use? There were more than five thousand people; what is the use of keeping five thousand peoples' keys and maintaining them unnecessarily? Once they have entered their dark cells, they have entered them forever.

The French revolutionaries naturally thought that the first thing that had to be done was to free the people from the Bastille. It is inhuman to put somebody for any act whatsoever into prison in a dark cell just to wait for his death, which might come fifty years afterwards, sixty years afterwards. Sixty years of waiting is an immense torture to the soul. It is not punishment, it is vengeance, revenge, because these people disobeyed the law. There is no balance between their acts and the punishment.

The revolutionaries opened the doors, they dragged people out from their dark cells. And they were surprised. Those people were not ready to get out of their cells.

You can understand. A person who has lived for sixty years in darkness—the sun is too much for him. He does not want to come out into the light, his eyes have become too delicate. And what is the point? He is now eighty; when he entered he was twenty. His whole life has been in this darkness. This darkness has become his home.

The revolutionaries wanted to make the prisoners free. They broke their chains, their handcuffs, because there were no keys. But the prisoners were very resistant. They did not want to go out of the prison. They said, "You don't understand our condition. A man who has been sixty years in this position, what will he do outside? Who will provide him food? Here food is given, and he can rest in his peaceful, dark cell. He knows he is almost dead. Outside he will not be able to find his wife, or what has happened to her; his parents will have died, his friends will have died, or may have completely forgotten him.

"And nobody is going to give him a job. A man who has been for sixty years out of work, who is going to give him a job? Not only that, this is a man from the Bastille, where the most dangerous criminals were kept—just the name of Bastille will be enough to have him refused from any job. Why are you forcing us? Where will we sleep? We don't have any houses. We have almost forgotten where we used to live, and by now somebody else must be living there. Our houses, our families, our friends, our whole world has changed so much in sixty years; we will not be able to make it. Don't torture us more. We have been tortured enough." There was reasonableness in what they were saying.

But revolutionaries are stubborn people; they won't listen. They forced them out of the Bastille, but by that night almost everybody had come back. They said, "Give us food because we are hungry." A few came in the middle of the night and they said, "Give us our chains back, because we cannot sleep without them. We have slept for fifty, sixty years with handcuffs, with chains on our legs, in darkness. They have become almost part of our bodies, we cannot sleep without them. You return our chains—and we want our cells. We were perfectly happy. Don't force your revolution on us. We are poor people. You can do your revolution somewhere else."

The revolutionaries were shocked. But the incident shows that freedom from is not necessarily a blessing.

You can see all over the world; countries have become free from the British Empire, from the Spanish empire, from the Portuguese empire—but their situation is far worse than it was when they were slaves. At least in their slavery they had become accustomed to it, they had dropped ambitions, they had accepted their situation as their destiny. Freedom from slavery simply creates chaos.

My whole family was involved in India's freedom struggle. They had all been to jail. Their education was disturbed. Nobody could graduate from the university because before they could pass the examination they were caught, and somebody was sent to jail for three years, somebody spent four years in jail. And then it was too late to start again, and they had become bona fide revolutionaries. In jail they contacted all the leaders of revolution; then their whole lives were devoted to revolution.

I was small, but I used to argue with my father, with my uncles: "I can understand that slavery is ugly, it dehumanizes you, humiliates you, it degrades you from the prestige of being a human being; it should be fought against. But my point is, what will you do when you are free? Freedom from is clear, and I am not against it. What I want to know and understand clearly is what you are going to do with your freedom.

"You know how to live in slavery. Do you know how to live in freedom? You know a certain order has to be maintained in slavery; otherwise you will be crushed, killed, shot. Do you know that in freedom it will be your responsibility to maintain the order? Nobody will be killing you and nobody else will be responsible for it—you have to be responsible for it. Have you asked your leaders what this freedom is for?"

I never received any answer. They said, "Right now we are so involved in getting rid of slavery; we will take care of freedom later on."

I said, "This is not a scientific attitude. If you are demolishing the old house, if you are intelligent you should at least prepare a map for the new house. The best would be that you prepare the new house before you demolish the old. Otherwise you will be without a house and then you will suffer—because it is better to be in the old house than to be without a house." In my family, great leaders of the Indian revolution used to stay with us—and this was my constant argument with them. I never found a single leader of the Indian revolution who had the answer to what they were going to do with freedom.

Freedom came. Hindus and Mohammedans killed each other in millions. They had been kept from killing each other by the British forces; the forces were removed, and there were riots all over India. Everybody's life was in danger. Whole towns were burning; whole trains were burning, and people were not allowed to get out of the trains.

I said, "This is strange. It was not happening in slavery, and it is happening in freedom—and the reason simply is that you were not prepared for what freedom is."

The country was divided into two parts—they had never thought about it— and in the whole country there was chaos. And the people who came to power had a certain expertise, and that expertise was in burning the bridges, burning the jails, killing the people who were enslaving the country. This expertise has nothing to do with building up a new country. But these were the leaders in the revolution; naturally they came to power. They had fought, they had won, and the power came into their hands. And it was in the wrong hands.

No revolutionary should be given the power—because he knows how to sabotage, but he does not know how to create; he only knows how to destroy. He should be honored, respected, given gold medals and everything, but don't give him power. You will have to find people who can be creative, but these will be the people who have not participated in revolution.

It is a very delicate matter.

Because the creative people were concerned with their creativity, they were not interested in who rules. Somebody must rule, but whether it is the Britishers, or whether it is the Indians doesn't matter to them. They were concerned with pouring their energy into their creative work, so they were not in the revolutionary ranks. Now, the revolutionaries will not allow them to have the power. In fact, they are the renegades. These are the people who never participated in revolution, and you are giving power to them?

So every revolution has failed in the world up to now, and for the simple reason that the people who make the revolution have one kind of expertise, and the people who can make a country, create a country, create responsibility in people, are a different lot. They don't participate in destruction, murder. But they cannot get to the power. Power goes into the hands of those who have been fighting. So, naturally, every revolution is intrinsically bound to fail.

Unless what I am saying is understood clearly.... There are two parts in revolution, *from* and *for*. And there should be two kinds of revolutionaries: those who are working for the first, that is, freedom *from*, and those who will work when the work of the first is finished, for freedom *for*.

But it is difficult to manage. Who will manage it? Everybody is full of lust for power. When the revolutionaries are victorious, the power is theirs; they cannot give it to anybody else. And the country will be in chaos. In every dimension it will fall lower and lower every day.

That's why I don't teach you revolution; I teach you rebellion. Revolution is of the crowd; rebellion is of the individual.

The individual changes himself. He does not care about the power structure; he simply manages to change his being, gives birth to a new man in himself. And if the whole country is rebellious... The most wonderful thing about it is that in rebellion, both kinds of revolutionaries can participate—because in rebellion, much has to be destroyed and much has to be created. Things have to be destroyed in order to create, so it has an appeal for both—those who are interested in destruction, and those who are interested in creativity.

It is not a crowd phenomenon. It is your own individuality. And if millions of people go through rebellion, then the power of countries, nations is going to be in the hands of these people, the rebels.

Only in rebellion can revolution succeed; otherwise, revolution has a split personality. Rebellion is one, single.

And when I say instead of revolution go for rebellion, I am bringing you closer to a complete whole. In revolution you are bound to be divided, either from something or for something. You cannot have both together, because they need different expertise.

But in rebellion both qualities are combined together.

When a sculptor makes a statue he is doing both; he is cutting the stone—destroying the stone as it was—and he is, by destroying the stone, creating a beautiful statue that was not there before. Destruction and creation go together, they are not divided.

Rebellion is whole. Revolution is half-half—and that is the danger of revolution. The word is beautiful, but down the centuries it has got connected with a split mind. And I am against all kinds of splits because they will drive you schizophrenic.

And if many people go through this rebellion—which is not against anybody, it is just against your own conditioning—and bring forth a new man within you, the problem is not difficult. Revolution should become out of date. Rebellion is the word for the future.

Two

Reform, Revolution, and Rebellion: The Three Rs of Man's Evolution

History centers around man's efforts to change society. This still goes on—what are we doing wrong?

Man's evolution passes through three stages: the reform, the revolution and the rebellion. The reform is the most superficial: it only touches the surface, it never goes more than skin-deep. It changes nothing but the dressing of man; it changes man's formalities. It gives man etiquette, manners—a kind of civilization—without changing anything essential in his being. It paints man, it polishes man, and yet deep down man remains the same. It is a delusion. It is fiction. It gives respectability, and makes everybody a hypocrite. It gives good manners, but they are against the inner core. The inner core has not even been understood.

But for the society, reform creates smoothness. It functions like a lubricant. It keeps the status quo going, it helps things remain the same—which will look paradoxical, because the reformist claims that he is changing society, but in fact all that he does is paint the old society in new colors. And the old society can exist more easily in new colors than it could have ever done with the old ones. The old were getting rotten, reform is a kind of renovation. The house is falling apart; the supports are falling, the foundations are shaking, and you go on giving new props to it, so you can keep the house from falling a little longer.

Reform is in the service of the status quo: it serves the past, not the future.

The second thing is revolution; it goes a little deeper. Reform only changes ideas, it does not even change policies. Revolution goes and touches the structure—but only the outer, not the inner.

Man has two structures, man lives on two planes. One is the physical, another is the spiritual. The revolution only goes to the physical structure, to the economic, to the political—they all belong to the physical. It goes deeper than reform, it destroys many old things, it creates many new things... but the being, the innermost being of man still remains unchanged. It creates morality, it creates character. Reform creates manners, etiquette, civilization: the formal behavior of the man is changed. Revolution changes man's outer structure—and really changes it, brings a new structure. But the inner blueprint remains the same, the inner consciousness is not touched. It creates a split.

The first, the reform, creates hypocrisy. The second, the revolution, creates schizophrenia, it makes the two structures of man unbridgeable. Man starts falling into two beings. The bridge is broken—that's why revolutionaries go on denying the soul. Marx and Engels and Lenin and Stalin and Mao, they all go on denying the soul. They have to deny it, they can't accept it, because if they accept it then their whole revolution seems to be very superficial; then their revolution is not total.

The reformist does not deny the soul, remember; he accepts it because it creates no problem for him—he never touches that point. That point is not a problem. Gandhi accepts the soul, Manu accepts the soul—they are reformists. They never say no to anything, they are people who go on saying yes; they are polite people. Unless it becomes absolutely necessary, they will not deny anything, they will accept. But revolutionaries deny the soul. They have to deny it, otherwise their revolution looks partial.

The third thing is rebellion. Rebellion is from the very essential core: it changes consciousness, it is radical; it transmutes, it is alchemical. It gives you a new being—not only a new body, not only new clothing, but a new being. A new man is born.

And in the history of consciousness there have been three types of thinkers: the reformer, the revolutionary and the rebel. Manu, Moses, Gandhi—these are reformers, the most superficial. John the Baptist, Marx, Freud—these are the revolutionaries. And Jesus, Buddha, Krishnamurti—these are the rebels.

To understand rebellion is to understand the heart of religion. Religion is rebellion. Religion is utter change. Religion is discontinuity with the past, the beginning of the new, the dropping of the old—totally. Nothing has to be continued, because if something continues it will keep the old alive.

Reform paints the surface. Revolution destroys the old, outer structure but the inner structure remains the same. In the Soviet Union or in China the inner man is the same, there is no difference, not a bit. The same mind—the same greedy, ambitious, egoistic mind; it is the same mind that is found in America or in capitalist countries, there is no difference in that mind. But the outer structure of the society has been changed, the outer structure of laws, state, economics, politics—that has been changed. Once the police force and the governmental power is taken away, man will fall back to his old pattern again. A Soviet society can be managed only by force, it cannot become democratic, because to allow people to be independent will be allowing them to bring their inner being again into their lives. That is still there. They have been prevented, they have been obstructed, they cannot live it; they have to live by what the government says. But they cannot live according to their being.

So, communism is basically dictatorial. It will remain dictatorial, because the fear is that if man is given freedom, then—because his consciousness is still there; the greed, the ambition, and all that has always been there is still there—that old consciousness will start working again. People will become rich, poor, powerful, powerless. People will start exploiting each other, people will start fighting for their ambitions. Those who are powerful in the Soviet Union will still be doing the same. Khrushchev used to brag about his cars, because he had so many. Nobody else could have them in Russia, but everybody wanted to have a car. It is just enforcement, not real revolution.

Real revolution is spontaneous. That revolution is called rebellion.

A few more distinctions between these three words, then you will be able to understand Jesus' approach.

Reform does not require much from you. It says, just make your front door beautiful; let the whole house be dirty. You live in dirt, but don't allow your neighbors to see your dirt. Just the front porch should be beautiful, because your neighbors are not interested in your inner being, in your inner house. They pass by the outside and they see only the front door. Do whatsoever you want, but do it from the back door. So the front door becomes a facade, a window, a showcase for the neighbors to see. You live from the back door really, you don't live from the front door. The front door is just there, artificial; you never enter through it, you never go out from it, it is there just to be seen by others.

Watch your front doors—everybody has them. They are called faces, masks, personalities because they are *persona*: lipstick, and powder and cosmetics. They give you a *persona*; you are not that, it is make-up.

Revolution goes a little deeper, but only a little deeper. It changes your drawing room so you can invite people to sit in your drawing room. In India it happens very much. In India the drawing room is beautiful, but don't go beyond that. People's kitchens are so dirty and ugly, their bathrooms are almost impossible. But in India nobody takes any care of the bathroom or the kitchen. The only care that is taken is of the drawing room; it is there where you meet your guests.

This is false; it does not touch your real being, but it keeps your prestige intact. That's what morality is, it is a beautiful drawing room. And if you can afford it, you can have a Picasso painting in your drawing room also. It depends on how much you can afford.

Just the other day I was reading a small story:

Charlie was taking his out-of-town pal, George, for a stroll through the city. They were admiring the scenery when George observed, "Say, will you look at that good-looking girl over there. She's smiling at us. Know her?"

"Yes, Betty—twenty dollars."

"And who is that brunette with her? Man, she's really stacked!"

"Dolores—forty dollars."

"Ah, but look what's coming! That's what I call really first-class."

"Gloria—eighty dollars."

"My God!" cried George. "Aren't there any nice, respectable girls in this town?"

"Of course," Charlie answered. "But you couldn't afford their rates."

Morality goes only so far; beyond that it stumbles and disappears. Everybody has his price. The moral man has a price. You watch yourself. If you are walking on the street and you find a thousand dollars, maybe you will not take them. But if you find ten thousand... then you hesitate, to take or not to take? But if you find one hundred thousand dollars, then there is no question, you take them! That shows how deep your morality is—one thousand, ten thousand, one hundred thousand; everybody has a price. One can only afford that much. Beyond that, it is too much, the morality is not worth it! Then you would like to choose the immoral.

The moral man is not totally moral; only a few layers of him are moral, beyond that, the immorality waits. So you can drive any moral person into immorality very easily. The only question is that you have to find his price.

I have heard that Mulla Nasruddin was traveling with a woman in a first-class compartment. They were alone. He introduced himself, and then he said, "Would you like to sleep with me tonight?"

The woman, who was really angry, said, "What do you think? Are you mad? What do you think of me? I am not a prostitute!"

Mulla said, "I will give you ten thousand rupees."

The woman started smiling, she came close, she was holding Mulla's hand.

And then Mulla said, "What about ten rupees?"

And the woman said, "Who do you think I am!"

Mulla said, "I know who you are. Now we are haggling over the price."

It is always a question of the price. Ten rupees, and the woman is angry. Ten thousand rupees and the woman is willing. And don't laugh at her, this is the situation of everybody! Morality does not transform you. It goes deeper than reform, it has a bigger price, but still, at the very core of your being, you remain the same.

Reform is partial revolution. Revolution is outer revolution. Rebellion is inner revolution. And only when the inner has happened, is it dependable; otherwise it is not dependable. Reform will make you a hypocrite, revolution will make you a schizophrenic. Only rebellion can give you your fullness of being, spontaneity, health, wholeness.

Reform will make you respectable. If you are after respect, then reform is enough. It will give you a plastic personality. From the outside you will start looking beautiful. On the inside you will be rotten and stinking, but nobody will be able to smell your stinking being; the plastic will protect you. Inside you will go on getting dirtier and dirtier, but on the outside you will keep a good face.

Revolution will create a split in you. It will make you a saint, but the sinner will be repressed. The sinner has not been absorbed into the saint, the sinner has been cut off. Revolution will make you two persons, it will create two worlds in you. The natural will be repressed, and the moral will be on top of it. The top dog, the moral, will try to control the underdog, the natural. And of course, the natural is very powerful because it is natural, so it will take revenge; it will go on sneaking into your life from the weak points. It will disrupt your morality, it will create guilt, and you will be in constant conflict because nobody can be victorious.

Your support, your intellectual support, is for the moral, but your whole being's support is for the natural. The moral is in the conscious and the natural is in the unconscious. The conscious is very small, and the unconscious is nine times stronger, nine times bigger than the conscious. But you only know the conscious, so in the conscious the morality will go on singing its song and in the unconscious, which is nine times more powerful, all kinds of immoralities will go on getting deeper roots in you. It will make you a saint *and* a sinner—the sinner will be repressed, and the sinner will wait for his time, for the right time to erupt, for the right time to take revenge.

That's why people look so sad, people look so dissipated, because their whole energy is going down the drain in the conflict. Continuous tension is there. The saint is very tense, he is always in anguish and always afraid—afraid of his own being that he has denied. And the denied is there! Sooner or later it will throw out the moralist, the egoist, the conscious pretender. It will overthrow the pretender.

Hence, the saint is always on the verge of a kind of insanity. And you know... if you try to be a saint, you will know that you are always on the verge. A small thing can change your whole balance, you can lose all your sanity. Neurosis breeds, grows, if you are split.

Rebellion is inner revolution. Rebellion starts from the "in," reform starts from the "out." Never start from the outside. Start from the innermost core. Start from your very being. Reform will tell you what to do. Revolution will tell you how to be—more saintly, of a better character, with good qualities. Revolution will make a hard crust around you, an armor that protects you from the outside, and from the inside too. A hard, steel armor—that is what is called "character."

A real man has no character. Jesus has no character, that was the problem; otherwise the Jews would not have been so against him. He was liquid; he had no character, he had no armor. He was open, vulnerable, defenseless, because he was not a moralist. He was not a saint, he was a sage.

Reform makes you a gentleman. Revolution makes you a saint. Rebellion makes you a sage. Jesus was a sage. Whatsoever he did was not done because of a certain morality, but because of a certain understanding; not because of rules given from the past, but because of a spontaneous awareness. Rebellion depends on awareness, revolution on character, reform on formalities.

Start by being more aware, then you start from the innermost. Let the light spread from there, so your whole being can be full of light. There is no way to go from the outside. The only way is to come from the inside—just like a seed grows from the inside, sprouts from the inside and becomes a big tree. Let that be your inner work too: like a seed, grow.

Reform is patchwork, a kind of whitewash—a little bit here, a little bit there, but the basic structure is not even touched. Reform can be for revolution or can be against revolution; it depends on you. There are two types of reformists: those who are preparing the ground for revolution, or those who are trying to prevent the revolution. Reform gives the feeling that things are getting better, so what is the need of creating a revolution? Why go to that much trouble? Reform gives hope, and people stop. So it depends on you.

A man of right understanding can use reform also, but a man who is not conscious will not be able to use reform as a process for revolution; on the contrary, reform will become a hindrance for revolution. And so is the case with revolution. Revolution can be a door to rebellion, but only with awareness; otherwise it becomes a hindrance. One thinks, "Now the revolution has happened, what is the need to go any deeper? It is already too much." So reform can either be a hindrance or a help, and so is the case with revolution.

All depends on your awareness, all depends on your understanding—how much you understand life.

So let this become one of the most fundamental rules of life and work, that everything ultimately depends on understanding, on how you understand. Even something that was going to become a great help can become a hindrance if understanding is missing. And even sometimes that which was going to be poisonous, with understanding can be changed into something medicinal. All medicines are made of poisons: they don't kill, they help people to remain healthy. In the right hands, even poison becomes medicine; and in the wrong hands, even medicine may prove to be a poison.

Revolution is the change of the structure—bodily, social, outer, economic, political; but man is not disturbed at all. It can be against rebellion or for rebellion. Out of one hundred, ninety-nine cases are against rebellion. That's why communism is so much against religion; it is not accidental.

Communism feels religion to be the real enemy. Why?—because religion goes far deeper than communism can ever go. That is the jealousy, that is the problem. If there is no religion, then communism seems to be the ultimate revolution. Then there is no higher. But if religion is there, then communism seems to be just so-so, lukewarm; it is not much to brag about. Communism wants to kill religion utterly, destroy religion from the earth. They have done that in the Soviet Union, they are doing it in China. They are doing it even in Tibet, which was one of the most religious countries, which had one of the most long-lived religions—alive, the purest; the spring was yet not dirty and polluted. Now they are destroying that too.

Communism is very much afraid of religion because communism can see the point that religion goes deeper, and it changes man from his very inner core. And only when the new human being is born, is a new society really born. We have tried all things. We have created ladies and gentlemen, and they didn't prove to be much. We have changed societies, we have tried utopias—they have all failed. Reform has failed, revolution has failed.

Rebellion has never been tried on a large scale. And whenever it has been tried on a small scale, it has always succeeded. With Buddha it succeeded: thousands of people went through a rebellion, became new. With Jesus it succeeded, with Lao Tzu it succeeded, with Krishna it succeeded. Success has always been with rebellion, but only for a very few people. It has never happened on a large scale. It has never gripped the soul of humanity. And that is where work is needed now.

The greater part of humanity has to be given the vision of awareness, rebellion, only then can man really become human. Man is only human for the name's sake; he is not yet human, because those humane qualities which make a man human are missing, are lacking. They are not there. Compassion is not there, love is not there, meditation is not there. The prayerfulness, the gratitude is not there, the celebration is not there.

Reform brings new ideas, revolution brings a new structure to support those new ideas, and rebellion brings new consciousness, a new man, a new being to support those structures. Start from the very foundation. Let rebellion be the foundation, then make the structure of revolution. And then on top of that, let there be a dome of reform, not otherwise. Otherwise the whole process will be topsy-turvy.

The basic thing is to understand the whole situation: how has man been doing up to now? what has been going wrong? why is there so much suffering? why do we always start from the wrong end and can never reach the real core of the problem?

Three

Priests and Politicians—Parasites in Power

Osho,

Why is humanity today becoming more and more miserable?

The cause is very simple, perhaps too simple. It is very close, very obvious, and this is the reason why most of the people go on missing it. When something is very obvious you start taking it for granted; when something is too close to your eyes you cannot see it. For seeing, some distance is needed.

So the first thing I would like you to remember is that it is not only today that humanity is miserable. It has always been miserable. Misery has almost become our second nature. We have lived in it for thousands of years. That closeness does not allow us to see it; otherwise it is so obvious.

But to see the obvious you need a child's vision, and we are all carrying thousands of years in our eyes. Our eyes are old; they cannot see afresh. They have already accepted things, and forgotten that those things are the very cause of misery.

The religious prophets, the political leaders, the moral lawgivers…you have respected them, not even suspecting that they are the cause of your misery. How can you suspect them? Those people have served humanity, sacrificed themselves for humanity. You worship them; you cannot relate them to your misery.

The causes of misery are camouflaged behind beautiful words, holy scriptures, spiritual sermons.

It happened when I was a student, the first prime minister of India came to visit the city. In Jabalpur, just in the middle of the city flows all the dirt of the city. The city is very big, and just in the middle of it all the waste of the city flows like a river. There is a bridge over it, and to pass over that bridge is to know something about hell. I have never seen any place so stinking.

The day Jawaharlal Nehru, the prime minister, came to visit the city, the bridge was one of the greatest problems. He had to cross it, that was the only way to get to the other part of the city. So they covered the bridge with mogra flowers. It was summertime, and the mogra is so fragrant a flower.... The whole bridge on both sides had garlands of mogra hanging. You could pass across the bridge and you would not be at all aware that just behind those mogras, the wall of flowers, was the dirtiest place possible.

I was just going to the university. Seeing people decorating the Naudra bridge—that was the name of the bridge; it was called Naudra because it had nine pillars, nine doors through which the dirt used to flow—seeing the people putting those flowers up, I stopped there. I started working with those people who were decorating, and nobody made any objection because many people were working, and it had to be done quickly, soon Jawaharlal was going to pass. So I got mixed in with the workers, the volunteers.

When Jawaharlal's procession came and he was standing in an open jeep, I stood in front of the jeep and stopped it. It would not have been possible in any other place because everywhere there were military police, guards, security. On

Naudra bridge these volunteers were on both sides, and there was no crowd, because nobody wanted to stand there. The crowd was not aware of what had happened, and that now those mogra flowers had completely covered the smell. The place was smelling of paradise! The people were not aware of it because nobody but the volunteers was near there.

I told Jawaharlal, "Please get down from the jeep. You have to look behind these flowers and see the reality of this city. You are being befooled; these flowers are not decorations for your welcome, they are put here to deceive you."

He said, "What do you mean?"

I said, "Get down, and just come close to the flowers and look beyond them." He was a very sensitive and intelligent man. Others tried to prevent him, the local leaders. I said, "Don't listen to these fools. These are the people who have arranged these flowers here. Have you seen in the city, anywhere, thousands of flowers arranged for your welcome? And here you don't see any crowd. The arithmetic is simple. Just come down."

He got down and went with me to look beyond the flowers: he could not believe it! He told the people, the local leaders, the mayor, the members of the municipal corporation and the president of the congress, "If this young man had not been so stubborn, I would have missed seeing the reality of your city. Is this what you have been doing here?"

He said to me, "If you come to New Delhi sometime, come and visit me."

I said, "Not 'sometime'—I will come simply to visit you. But tell the idiots surrounding you that I am allowed in."

He told his secretary, "You have to take care that nobody prevents him." That's how that secretary became one of my disciples. And whenever I needed something, he was immediately ready to arrange it; the doors of Jawaharlal's house were always open for me.

I remembered this incident because that's what has happened with the whole of humanity. You see the misery, but you don't see the cause. The cause is covered with flowers. You see the flowers, and because flowers cannot cause the misery, you turn back.

The second thing to remember is that it is not only now that humanity is miserable; it has always been so.

Yes, one thing new has happened—it is a little difference, but a difference that really makes a difference—and that is, a certain percentage of humanity has now become more aware than it has ever been before. Misery has always been there; but to be aware of the misery, that is a new factor. And that is the beginning of transformation.

If you become aware of something, then there is a possibility that something can be done to change it. People have lived in misery, accepting it as part of life, as their destiny. Nobody has questioned it. Nobody has asked why.

And before anybody could ask why, the religious prophets, messiahs and priests were ready with the answer.

Christianity is ready with the answer: it is because Adam and Eve committed the original sin; hence you are suffering. Now, can you see any connection? Even according to Christianity, the world was created four thousand and four years before Jesus' birth—which is not at all accurate, which is absolutely stupid. The world is millions of years old.

But even if the Christians are right, Adam still must have committed the original sin at least five thousand years ago. Somebody committing a sin five thousand years ago...how many generations have passed since then? And you are still miserable because of his sin? That seems to be absolutely unjust! If he did commit the sin, God made him suffer, so why should you be suffering? You were never a part of it. If anybody has to suffer, it should be God himself, because in the first place what was the need of creating those two trees? If man was not allowed to eat from them, it would have been so simple—God should not have created those two trees. He was committing the original sin, if anybody was.

Then, even if God had created those trees, what was the need to tell Adam not to eat from them? I don't think that Adam on his own, even by now, would have found those two trees. Among the millions of trees, it would have been just a coincidence if Adam had found them. But God showed him the trees, saying, "These are the two trees, and you are not to eat from them."

And this God is Jewish. Sigmund Freud understands it better—he is also Jewish, born out of the original sin—he understands far better than this Jewish God. To tell somebody not to do something is to provoke them, is to give them a challenge, is to make the person fascinated. It is not the snake who really persuades Adam and Eve, it is God's "don't" that provokes them, and they become curious about why.

And the trees are not poisonous. One tree is the tree of wisdom. There seems to be no logic in why the tree of wisdom should be prohibited to man. And the other tree is of eternal life. Both trees are the best in the whole garden of Eden. God should have told him, "Don't miss these two trees! Anything else you can miss, but these two trees you should not miss." On the contrary, He says to Adam and Eve, "Don't do this."

That "don't" is the real cause of their disobeying; the serpent is just an excuse.

But even if they did commit the sin, whether through God or through the serpent, it is absolutely certain that you are not part of it—in no way! You were not there to support them.

The Christians have been befooling the whole world, the Jews have been befooling the whole world, saying that it is because of the original sin that man is suffering, he is in misery. He has to turn back, he has to undo what Adam and Eve did. They disobeyed; you have to obey God. Just as they disobeyed and were thrown out of heaven, if you obey totally, without any doubt, without any questioning, you will be allowed back into the world of bliss, paradise.

Misery exists because of the original sin, according to these Judaic religions: Judaism, Christianity, Mohammedanism. These three religions have come from the same source; they all believe in the same original sin, and that we are suffering because we are the progeny of those same people who committed it. Even human justice cannot punish a criminal's son because he is a criminal's son. His father may have murdered somebody, a major crime, but then you cannot punish the son, too. The son has nothing to do with it.

Adam and Eve did not commit any major crime—they just had a little curiosity. And I think anybody who had any sense would have done the same. It was absolutely certain to happen, because there is a deep need in man to know. It is intrinsic, it is not sin. It is in the very nature of human beings to know. And God is prohibiting them. He is saying, "Remain ignorant."

There is, in the same way, an intrinsic, intense desire for eternal life. Nobody wants to die. Even the person who commits suicide is not against life. Perhaps he is hoping the next life will be better. He is so tired of all this suffering and anguish that he thinks, "In this life there is no hope, so why not take a chance? This life is not giving you anything and is not going to give you anything—take the chance! If you survive and enter into another life, perhaps...." That "perhaps," that lingering desire, is still in the man who is committing suicide. He may be committing suicide against many things, but he is not committing suicide against life itself.

These two things, the desire to know and the desire for life, are the basic and the most deeply rooted desires in man, and yet he is prohibited from fulfilling his own nature. His nature is condemned as criminal, as a nature which is rooted in sin. If he fulfills it, he feels guilty; if he does not fulfill it, he will remain miserable.

These people have created the background of your misery.

Let me summarize it: if you are natural you will feel guilty. Then that will be your misery, your anxiety, your anguish—what punishment there is going to be for you! You are disobeying God, because all your scriptures and their commandments are against your nature. So if you fulfill your nature, there is misery. If you don't fulfill your nature, there is bound to be misery because then you will be empty, unfulfilled, discontented; you will feel futile, utterly meaningless.

So there are two types of miserable people in the world: one who follows the religious prophets, and one who does not follow them. It is very difficult to find a third category, a man like me, who does not care a bit. I neither follow them nor am I against them. I do not even hate them; there is no question of loving them. To me they are absolutely absurd and meaningless, irrelevant to our existence. Take either side and you will be in trouble. Don't take sides, either for or against; just tell those guys, "Go to hell! And take all your scriptures with you." Only then can you be free of misery.

In the East they have a different explanation. Explanations can be different, but the purpose is the same. In the East, the three religions—Hinduism, Jainism, Buddhism—all teach that your misery is because of bad actions in past lives. And you have lived millions of past lives, in different shapes, different bodies, animals, birds.... In that way, they have a vast perspective. Eight hundred and forty million species of life exist. At least their perspective is vast, not small like the Christian perspective...only six thousand years?

The Eastern perspective is certainly great: eight hundred and forty million species, and you have passed through them all; then you have become a human being. In all these long years—you will have to use the word "light years" with Hindus and Jainas and Buddhists—you have committed so many things, good and bad, and everything is recorded with you. If you are suffering, that simply means your bad actions are heavy on you. You have to suffer, that is the only way to get rid of them. You have to pay for your actions. Who else is going to pay? You murdered somebody in your last life, now who is going to pay?

Their explanation seems more mathematical, more logical, than Adam committing sin and you suffering six thousand years afterwards. So many generations have passed, and still the sin is fresh. So many generations have suffered and been punished for it, and you are still being punished for it. Can you punish so many people for one man's sin? And this is going to go on forever and forever. At least the Eastern vision seems to be more logical: that in your past life you have committed some bad actions, and of course you have to suffer for them. I say it looks more logical, but it is not existentially true.

What do I mean when I say it is not existentially true? I mean that whenever you act, the result of the act is intrinsic in the act itself, it does not wait for the next life. Why should it wait? If you drink poison now, will you die in the next life? I have been arguing with Hindu shankaracharyas, Jaina monks, Buddhist bhikkus, saying "Tell me, if somebody hits his hand with a hammer, will he suffer in the next life or here, right now?" Action brings its reaction immediately. It does not wait. Why should it wait, and why for the next life particularly?

They have been befooling people, of course more logically than Christians and Jews and Mohammedans. Hence, no sophisticated Hindu can be converted to Mohammedanism, Judaism, Christianity—impossible, because all your ideas look very childish; he has far more logical explanations. But those logical explanations are only significant on the surface; deep down there is nothing much in them.

I have argued with all these people. Not a single one has been able to answer my question. If you put your arm in the fire, will you be burned in the next life? The action is here, the reaction has to be here. They are joined together, they cannot be separated. The moment you love, you are happy. It is not that in this moment you love, and you are in deep misery now, and in the next life, whether there you love or not, suddenly one day you will feel happy—the good karma of your last life! You are disconnecting things that are not, in the nature of things, in any way possible to disconnect. You hate somebody and in that very hatred you are burning in fire. You are angry and in that very anger, not outside of it, you suffer. My approach is that each moment, whatsoever you are doing you are getting the immediate reaction.

Man is in misery because religions have not helped him to destroy the causes of misery. On the contrary, they have consoled him so that he remains as he is. In the East, they have told people that revolt, revolution, are of the same order as disobedience, disorder, creating chaos: you will suffer tremendously in the coming life. You are suffering now, and you are preparing the ground for more suffering. So they created this gap between this life and the coming life, the past life and this life. And it is a beautiful strategy, because neither have you any evidence of your past life—that you committed any bad actions or good actions—nor have you any way to know what is going to happen to you in the next life, the coming life. They have given beautiful explanations and camouflaged the whole stinking reality behind beautiful flowers. So you smell the flower and you forget the stinking river just flowing underneath, an undercurrent. Throw away these flowers and immediately you will be able to see why humanity is in so much suffering.

The new thing that has happened is, as I said before, that one percent of humanity has come to a point where it can become a little alert, awake. And that one percent of humanity, becoming aware of the misery, seeing the whole of humanity already in hell, is asking, "What other hell are you talking about? There cannot be anything worse than what is happening on the earth." This one percent of humanity has created such questions. Those questions have also reached those people who are not alert, but the questions have reached them anyway. They have also heard and started feeling some little stirring of consciousness: "Yes, there is misery, and immense misery."

Politicians have been deceiving you. They say, "If there is democracy, there will be no suffering. If there is independence, there will be no suffering. If there is socialism, there will be no suffering. If there is communism, suffering disappears." But there is democracy, and suffering goes on growing, accumulating. Countries are independent, all countries are not in slavery, but even in the countries that are independent, the misery is not less. Perhaps it is even more, because they cannot dump their misery on anybody else —now they are independent. A slave country at least has a consolation. That is my experience.

Before India became independent there was such a feeling all over India. My house was a place of conspiracy. My two uncles had been in jail many times, and every week they had to go to the police station to report that they were not doing anything against the government, and that they were still there. They were not allowed to move out of the town but people were coming to them—and they all had so much hope.

I was a small child but I always wondered, "These people are saying that just by becoming independent, all misery will disappear. How can it happen? I don't see any connection." But there was hope. There was the promised land, very close by; just a little struggle and you would reach it. There was suffering, but you were not responsible for it: the Britishers were responsible. It was a great consolation to dump everything on the Britishers.

In fact, I used to ask these revolutionaries who used to visit my house secretly, or sometimes stay in my house for months.... One of them, a very famous revolutionary, Bhavani Prasad Tiwari, was the national leader of the socialist party. Whenever he had to go underground he used to come to my village and just live in my house, hidden. For the whole day he would not come out—and nobody knew him in the village anyway. But I was after him. He told me again and again, "You bring such inconvenient questions that sometimes I think it would be better to be in a British jail than in your house! At least there I would get first class treatment."

He was a famous leader so he would have got first class treatment—political prisoners' special class—with all the facilities, good food, good library. And at least he would get freedom, because first class prisoners were not forced to do any labor. They would write their autobiographies and other books: all the great books these great Indian leaders have written were written in jails. And they would go for walks—they were put in beautiful places that were not even jails; they were created especially for them. They had acres of greenery, beautiful views. So Bhavani Prasad Tiwari used to say to me, "It would be better if I stop going underground, because you ask such inconvenient questions."

I said, "If you cannot answer them, what is going to happen to the country when the country becomes independent? These will be the questions you will have to solve. You cannot even answer them verbally, and then you will have to actually solve them. I asked him, "Just by the Britishers leaving the country"—and there were not many Britishers—how is poverty going to disappear? And do you want me to believe that before the Britishers came to India, India was not poor?

"It was as poor as it is now, perhaps even poorer, because the Britishers brought industry, technology, and that helped the country to become a little better. They brought education, schools, colleges, universities. Before that, there was no way to be educated: the only educated people were the Brahmins, because the father would teach the son. They kept everybody else uneducated because that was the best way to keep them enslaved. Education can become dangerous.

"How are you going to destroy poverty? How are you going to destroy the hundreds of kinds of anxieties and miseries which have nothing to do with the British? Now, a husband is suffering because of his wife—how is it going to help? The Britishers have gone, okay; but the wife will still be there, the husband will still be there—how is it going to change anything?"

He said, "I know it is very difficult, but let us first get independence."

Political leaders have kept humanity hoping—always somewhere far away, the great hope....

For the classless society the Soviet Union has suffered everything for sixty years: "The classless society is going to happen soon!" When will those days of waiting be finished? This is an old strategy. Jesus used to say to his followers, "Very soon you will be with me in the kingdom of God. Very soon you will see that those who follow me are saved, and those who don't follow me fall into eternal hell." It has not happened yet, and we don't even know whether Jesus is with God or not.

He even promised that he would be coming back. I think he must have lost courage—once crucified is enough! Now again he will be crucified, this time in the Vatican, because this time he will be coming as a Christian. And the pope will be the person who will decide: "This man has to be crucified—he is a pretender, an antichrist. He is not our lord, because when our lord comes he will come with glory, sitting on a cloud. That's how the lord has to come. And this man is born out of a woman, and not even out of a virgin." They are looking for the cloud the lord will be coming on, and the lord has escaped!

But the hope.... Politicians go on giving hope and nothing materializes.

One thing has to be understood clearly: no hope is going to help, no false explanation is going to help. You have to put aside all this crap and see into reality as it is.

Four

Christianity and Communism: Partners in the Same Racket to Exploit the Poor

Osho,

You talk so much against the religions, but why do you seem to be especially against Christianity?

I hate to favor Christianity with any special attention but unfortunately it deserves it. It is the ugliest manifestation of religion on the earth, for many reasons.

The first: Christianity is the only well-organized religion. The more a religion is well-organized, the less is the possibility of its being a religion. Truth, by its very nature, cannot be organized. To organize truth or to kill it means the same thing.

Truth is alive when organization is only functional, loose. Christianity's organization is very tight, bureaucratic, hierarchical. Because of this kind of organization, it has become more a game of power politics than the flowering of religious qualities.

In the past two thousand years Christianity has done more harm to humanity than any other religion. Mohammedanism has tried to compete with it, but has not been successful. It came very close, but Christianity still remains on the top. It has slaughtered people, burned people alive. In the name of God, truth, religion, it has been killing and slaughtering people—for their own sake, for their own good. And when the murderer is murdering you for your own good, then he has no feeling of guilt at all. On the contrary, he feels he has done a good job. He has done some service to humanity, to God, to all the great values of love, truth, freedom. He feels excited. He feels that he is now a better human being.

When crimes are being used for people to feel like better human beings, that is the worst that can happen to anybody. Now he will be doing evil, thinking it is good. He will be destroying good, thinking it is good. This is the worst kind of indoctrination that Christianity has put into people's minds. The idea of the crusade, of a religious war, is a great contribution of Christianity. Mohammedanism learned it from Christianity; they cannot claim to be the originators of the idea. They call it jihad, holy war, but they came five hundred years later than Jesus. Christianity had already created in people's minds the idea that a war too can be religious.

Now, war as such is irreligious. There cannot be anything like a crusade, a jihad, a holy war. If you call war holy, then what is left to be called unholy? This is a strategy to destroy people's thinking. The moment they think of *crusade*, they don't think there is anything wrong: they are fighting for God against the devil. And there is no God and no devil—you are simply fighting and killing people. And what business is it of yours anyway? If God cannot destroy the devil, do you think you can? If God is impotent and cannot destroy the devil, then can some Polack pope do it? Can these Christians do it? Can Jesus do it? And for eternity God has lived with the devil. Even now, the forces of evil are far more powerful than the forces of good, for the simple reason that the forces of good are also in the hands of the forces of evil.

Calling war religious, holy, is the cause of war—because the first world war happened in the Christian context, the second world war happened in the Christian context, and the third world war is going to happen in the Christian context. There are other religions also, but why did these two great wars happen in the Christian context? Christianity cannot save itself from taking the responsibility. Once you create the idea that war can be holy then you cannot monopolize the idea.

Adolf Hitler was saying to his people, "This war is holy"; it was a crusade. He was simply using Christianity's contribution. He was a Christian, and he believed himself to be the reincarnation of the prophet, Elijah. He thought himself equal to Jesus Christ, perhaps better, because what Jesus could not do, he was trying to do. All that Jesus succeeded in doing was getting crucified. Adolf Hitler was almost successful. If he had succeeded—which was ninety-nine percent possible, just by one percent he missed—then the whole world would have been purified of all that is Jewish, of all that is non-Christian. What would have remained?

And do you know?—Adolf Hitler was blessed by the German archbishop, who told him, "You are going to win because Christ is with you and God is with you." And the same fools were blessing Winston Churchill, saying, "God is with you and Christ is with you, you are sure to win." The same fools, even bigger ones, were in the Vatican, because the Vatican is just part of Rome, and Mussolini was being blessed by the pope—a representative, an infallible representative, of Jesus Christ.

One can think the German archbishop is not infallible, the archbishop of England is not infallible—we can forgive them, they are fallible people—what about the pope, who for centuries has been claimed by the Christians to be infallible? Now, this infallible pope blesses Mussolini for victory because "he is fighting for Jesus Christ and God"—and Mussolini and Adolf Hitler were one party; together they were trying to win the whole world.

Perhaps the pope was hoping that if Mussolini wins then Christianity will have a chance to become the universal religion. They have been trying for two thousand years to make Christianity the universal religion, to destroy all other religions. It is not only that Christianity has contributed to the idea of war....

In Jainism there is no question of holy war. Every war is unholy. You may be fighting in the name of religion, but fighting itself is irreligious. Buddhism has no idea of any holy war; hence, Jainism and Buddhism have never contributed to any single war, and their history is very long. Jainism at least for ten thousand years has been in existence and has not had a single war, holy or unholy. Buddhism is also older than Christianity, five hundred years older, and has as big a membership as Christianity—because except India, the whole of Asia is Buddhist—but there has not been a single instance of any Buddhist priest blessing any kind of war.

Wars have been there; politicians have been there in those countries too. They have been fighting—Japan and China have been fighting and both are Buddhist—but neither Japanese Buddhist priests nor Chinese Buddhist priests were in any way involved, not even by giving a blessing. These people show a little bit of courage. And the pope seems to be absolutely hocus-pocus. He has no guts.

In India, a few years back, China attacked India. For the first time in the whole history of India, a Jaina acharya, head of one of the Jaina sects, blessed the government, the Indian government. His name is Acharya Tulsi.

I had to fight against him, criticizing him; I went all over the country telling people, "This man should be defrocked and removed from his position because he has committed a crime for which, in ten thousand years, no single Jaina priest has ever been blamed. This man is a politician, this man is not religious."

I talked to Acharya Tulsi and I told him, "If you had any sense of dignity you would resign, because you have acted like a politician. What business was it of yours? Who has asked you to bless India against China? For a religious man, political boundaries should not mean anything. India is yours, China is yours; and if they are fighting, let them fight. You should rather pray that this war stops, that some wisdom comes to these fools—both parties. That would be religious." And I told him, "You are acting more like a Christian pope than like a Jaina priest."

He was angry with me, but he had no substantial argument. But I told him, "Blessing India shows simply that you are not a man who joins the universal consciousness, you live within boundaries." But this is the only instance of Jaina involvement in politics, and no Hindu shankaracharya has ever blessed a war.

Now, Christianity deserves all the credit for making war, the most ugly thing in human life, holy. And then behind the name of a crusade you can do everything: rape women, burn people alive, kill innocent children, old people, anything. This is a blanket term, a cover: a holy war, a "crusade." But what actually happens behind it? All atomic weapons, nuclear weapons, are produced in the Christian context.

It is not that the world lacks intelligence. If China can produce Confucius, Lao Tzu, Chuang Tzu, Mencius, Lieh Tzu, there is no reason why China cannot produce an Albert Einstein, a Lord Rutherford. There is no reason at all, because Chuang Tzu, Lieh Tzu, Lao Tzu, Mencius, Confucius—any of them is a thousandfold wiser than Jesus or Moses. They are simply pygmies compared to these people. If such geniuses can be created by China, then there is no reason why China cannot create atomic scientists. And do you know, China was the first in creating the printing press? In China the printing press has been in existence for three thousand years.

In India, if they can produce a man like Patanjali, who single-handedly has produced the whole system of yoga; if they could produce Gautam the Buddha, Mahavira the Jaina, Shankara, Nagarjuna—great philosophers; there is no one comparable from the West, not a single person can be held up in comparison to Gautam Buddha. And it is not only philosophers. If you compare Patanjali of five thousand years ago with any physiologist of today, you will find that the physiologist knows nothing compared to Patanjali.

Three thousand years ago in India, Sushrut, a great physician and surgeon, existed. In his books he describes the most intricate surgery that is possible only today—even brain surgery, and with all the instruments. If these people could produce that, what was missing? Why were they not trying to produce atom bombs? India produced mathematics, without which no science is possible. That's why in all the languages you still follow the Indian digital system, because it was produced first in India: the numbers one, two, three, four, five, six, seven, eight, nine, ten. All these numbers in all the languages come from Sanskrit.

Seven thousand years ago they created the basis of mathematics, but they never used their mathematical understanding for destructive purposes. They used it for creative purposes because no religion there was giving them the incentive to war. All religions were saying war is ugly, about that there was no dispute, and those countries were not going to support any program, any project, any research, which was going to lead them into war.

The first astronomical book was written in India four thousand years ago. Those people were far ahead of the West. Four thousand years ago the West did not even have a single name to mention. The greatest names in the West are not more then twenty-five centuries old. Perhaps with Socrates your greatest name happens, but Socrates was three or four thousand years later. What he said had already been said, and what he thought he was contributing to thought was not new. Of course, to him it was new because he was unaware that somewhere people had already talked about this, and had gone very deep into it.

I am saying this to make it clear to you that it is Christianity which is responsible for giving science the incentive to war. If Christianity had created an atmosphere of nonviolence, and had not called war holy, then we would have avoided these two world wars; and without those two, certainly the third could not happen. Those two are absolutely necessary steps for the third; they have led you already toward the third. You are geared for it, and there is no possibility to come back, to turn back.

Not only has science been corrupted by Christianity, Christianity itself has given birth to strange ideologies, either directly, or as a reaction. In both ways it is responsible. Poverty has existed in the world for thousands of years, but communism is a Christian contribution. And don't be misguided by the fact that Karl Marx was a Jew, because Jesus was also a Jew. If a Jew can create Christianity.... The context of Karl Marx is Christian, it is not Jewish. The idea was given by Jesus Christ. The moment he said, "blessed are the poor for they shall inherit the kingdom of God," he sowed the seed of communism.

Nobody has said it so straight, because to say it so straight you need a crazy man like me, who can call a spade not only a spade but a fucking spade! What is there in just calling a spade a spade? Once Jesus created the idea that "Blessed are the poor for they shall inherit the kingdom of God," it was child's play to change it to the more practical and pragmatic communism. What Marx says in essence is, "blessed are the poor for theirs is the earth." He is simply changing some spiritual jargon into practical politics.

"Kingdom of God"—who knows whether it exists or not? But why waste this opportunity when you can have the kingdom of earth? The whole of communism is based on that single statement of Jesus. It is just a little turn, throwing away the esoteric nonsense and bringing practical politics into it. Yes, blessed are the poor because theirs is the whole kingdom of this earth—that's what Karl Marx is saying.

Strange, that nowhere else—in the context of Buddhism, Hinduism, Jainism, Sikhism, Taoism or Confucianism—does communism appear; it appears only in the context of Christianity. It is not just accidental, because you can see fascism also appears in the context of Christianity. Socialism, Fabian socialism, Nazism—all are Christian children, kids of Jesus Christ. Either directly influenced by him... because he is the man who says, "In my kingdom of God, a camel can pass through the eye of a needle but a rich man cannot enter through the gates." What do you think about this man? Is he not a communist? If he is not a communist, then who is? Even Karl Marx, Engels, Lenin, Stalin or Mao Tse-tung, have not made that strong a statement: A rich man cannot enter into the kingdom of God. And you see the comparison he makes? It is possible for a camel—this is impossible—to pass through the eye of a needle; he says even that is possible, but the entrance of a rich man into the kingdom of God is impossible. If it is impossible there, why leave them here? Make it impossible here, too! That's what Marx did.

In fact, what theoretically Jesus offered, Marx gave a practical turn. But the original theoretician was Jesus. Karl Marx may not have even recognized it, but in no other context is communism possible. In no other context is Adolf Hitler possible. In India if you want to declare yourself a man of God, you cannot be an Adolf Hitler. You cannot even participate in politics, you cannot even be a voter. You cannot destroy millions of Jews, or millions of people belonging to other religions and still claim that you are a reincarnation of an ancient prophet, Elijah.

In India there have been thousands of people declaring that they are incarnations, that they are prophets, *tirthankaras*, but they have to prove it by their lives, too. Maybe they are phony, most of them are—but even then, nobody can be an Adolf Hitler and still say that he is a prophet, that he is a religious man.

I received a threatening letter from somewhere in America. I had never thought about it, that there is, in America, a Nazi party. The president of the American Nazi party wrote a letter to me saying, "We have been hearing you speak against Adolf Hitler and that hurts our religious feelings." I am rarely amazed, but I was amazed: their religious feelings! "Because to us, Adolf Hitler is the prophet Elijah, and we hope that you will not hurt our religious feelings in the future."

I told my secretary, "Now I am especially going to hurt them more. I was not aware of that, that religious feelings are hurt by speaking about or criticizing Adolf Hitler." You cannot think of this happening in India or China or Japan—impossible. But in a Christian context it is possible: not only possible, it has already happened. And if Hitler had won the war, all these Americans and all these Russians and all these British people would be worshipping him as God. He would have been proclaimed as having overcome the world and changed the whole of humanity into Christianity. And he would have changed it; he had the power.

What power did poor Jesus have? He could not even save himself. Adolf Hitler winning the war would have certainly changed the whole world into Christianity. But that Christianity would not have been the Christianity of Jesus Christ; it would have been the Christianity of Adolf Hitler. The Bible would not have been the holy book any more; Hitler's autobiography, *Mein Kampf*, would have been the holy book.

I am not paying special attention to Christianity, but it deserves it. It has done so much harm, so much nuisance. It is impossible to believe that people still go on keeping it alive. The churches should be demolished, the Vatican should be completely removed. There is no need of these people. Whatever they have done they have done wrong. Other religions have also done wrong, but proportionately they are nothing compared to Christianity.

It has been exploiting the poverty of people to convert them to Christianity. Yes, Buddhism has converted people, but not because people were hungry and you provided them food, and because you provided them food they started feeling obliged to you. If you provide them clothes, if you provide them other facilities, education for their children, hospitals for their sick people, naturally they feel obliged. And then you start asking them, "What has Hinduism done for you? What has Buddhism done for you?"

Naturally, Buddhism, Hinduism and Jainism have never opened a hospital, a school; they have never done any such service. This is the only argument. And those people are so obliged that they feel certainly no other religion has been of any help to them, and they become Christians. This is not an honest way, this is bribing people. This is not conversion, this is buying people because they are poor. You are taking advantage of their poverty. The poor have been there always; but to exploit their poverty to increase your population is sheer politics—ugly, mean. Politics is a game of numbers. How many Christians you have in the world, that is your power. The more Christians there are, the more power is in the hands of Christian priests, the priesthood.

Nobody is interested in saving anybody, but just in increasing the population. What Christianity has been doing is continually issuing orders from the Vatican against birth control, saying it is sin to use birth control methods; it is sin to believe in abortion or to propagate abortion, or to make it legal. Do you think they are interested in the unborn children? They are not interested, they have nothing to do with those unborn children. They pursue their interest knowing perfectly well that if abortion is not practiced, if birth control methods are not practiced, then this whole humanity is going to commit a global suicide. And it is not so far away that you cannot see the situation. Within just fifteen years the world population will be such that it will be impossible to survive. Either you will have to go into a third world war...which will be a safer method. People will die more quickly, more easily, more comfortably with nuclear weapons than with hunger, because hunger can keep you alive for ninety days, and those ninety days will be really a torture.

But the Vatican has come out with a long message to humanity: "Abortion is sin. Birth control is sin." Now, nowhere in the Bible is abortion sin. Nowhere in the Bible is birth control sin, because no birth control was needed. Out of ten children, nine were going to die. That was the proportion, and that was the proportion in India just a few decades ago: out of ten children, only one would survive. That was perfectly okay. Then the population was not too great, not too heavy on the resources of the earth. Now, even in India, out of ten children, only one dies.

So on one hand medical science goes on helping people to survive, and Christianity goes on opening hospitals and distributing medicines, and Mother Teresa is there to praise you and the pope is going to bless you. There are all kinds of associations—in America, there is a Christian association called "Underground Evangelism," which works in communist countries to distribute Bibles freely and to distribute these stupid ideas that abortion is sin and birth control is sin.

Now, from where do these popes get the idea that it is sin? It is not in the Bible, it is not in any old scriptures. Has the pope got a new message from God? Some amendment to the Bible? Should these Vatican declarations be added to the Bible as the fifth gospel? What do they want? And who are they to decide that birth control is sin? The pope says once a child is conceived, if abortion happens then, that child dies. That can be understood, but at what point can the child be counted as alive? At one week can you say he is alive, he is a human being? At two weeks, three weeks? At what point does he become a human being? You have to decide at what point the child is a human being, because in the beginning he looks just like a fish, he even has a tail— and you are eating fish and animals without any trouble!

What these people are suggesting about birth control and abortion is absolutely foolish. You cannot decide what time the child becomes a human being. And if it can be decided, it has to be decided by physiologists, medical people.

But what is wrong in birth control? Because then no conception happens. And if the pope says that too is wrong because you are preventing a conception from happening, then he has to also declare that each time you make love, if conception does not happen, then you are committing a sin. You follow my idea? Because whether you use birth control methods or not, every time you make love, conception does not happen. All those times that conception does not happen, remember, will be counted as sin. He is asking you why the conception did not happen— it has to happen.

His whole interest is in bringing many more children into the world, many more orphans into the world. Make it so overcrowded, so poor, that Christianity can become the universal religion. That has been their ambition for two thousand years. It has to be exposed. This ambition is inhuman; and if I have been criticizing Christianity it is not without reason

The most important thing is that I am speaking within a Christian context. If I were speaking in a Hindu context, I would not be criticizing Christianity, I would be criticizing

Hinduism, or in a Buddhist context I would be criticizing Buddhism. It would be useless to criticize Christianity in a Buddhist context because those people would love it.

I am a person who impresses people and creates enemies, not friends—that is not my policy. I would love the whole world to be my enemy. But all these people are so cowardly that they cannot honestly even accept that they are enemies. Every day dozens of letters are received; they are praying for me, that God should forgive me. These fools! They should pray to me that I should forgive God and them. Why should God forgive me? If there is going to be any trouble I am ready to take it.

One thing is certain: whether God forgives me or not, I am not going to forgive him. So they should pray to me, not to God. They don't understand what they are saying. They go on writing letters, "We pray to God that he should forgive you for what you are saying."

There is no God.

I am speaking against nobody.

That's why I am enjoying it, because if there *were* a God do you think I would enjoy it? It would be trouble. It is sheer enjoyment—no trouble at all.

Five

Dictatorship is the Power in Their Hands

Osho,

All my life, I did what I was told. Now, it seems, it is all up to me... But who am I to know what to do? By the way, I'm German.

Even without your saying it, I would have known you are a German!

All the dictators in the world are created by us because we want somebody else to tell us what to do. There is a very subtle reason for it: when you are told by somebody else what to do, you don't have any responsibility for whether it is right or wrong. You are free of responsibility; you don't have to think about it; you don't have to be worried about it. The whole responsibility goes to the person who is giving you the orders to do something.

People like Adolf Hitler or Joseph Stalin or Ronald Reagan are not in their powerful positions just because of some quality of theirs. They are there because millions of people want to be told what to do—without anybody dictating to them, they are at a loss. We create the dictators.

Adolf Hitler was almost crazy but a whole nation, one of the most intelligent nations in the world, which has created a great tradition of philosophers, thinkers, theologians of the first rate... Germany has produced people like Martin

Heidegger, who is perhaps the twentieth century's greatest philosopher—but he was also a follower of Adolf Hitler. It seems almost incomprehensible for a man of the qualities of Martin Heidegger. I have looked into all the philosophers of the world; Martin Heidegger seems to have such a genius, such a great originality in approaching things from absolutely new directions—but he was a follower of Adolf Hitler; he supported him! I was wondering what could be the reason that he, and the whole nation, supported that madman. The reason is that nobody wants to have any responsibility. But the moment you lose your responsibility, you think it is a burden and somebody else takes it, you also lose your individuality; you also lose your freedom.

Your responsibility is not separate from your freedom, your individuality. Once you drop your responsibility on somebody else's shoulders, you have reduced yourself to a nonentity. Of course, now nobody will blame you if something goes wrong, but you have lost your soul.

People condemn the dictators, but nobody thinks about what the psychology is, how dictators are created, who creates them. We are the people who create them, and we create them in the hope that they will take the responsibility. But we are not aware that with the responsibility goes our freedom, goes our individuality, goes democracy, goes freedom of thinking or expression—everything. We have lost our soul the moment we put our responsibility into somebody else's hands. And there are people who enjoy to dominate, to dictate; these are insane people.

So it is a strange situation. People want to be unburdened of responsibility, and of course there are a few people who are ready to take all the responsibilities because they are also taking all your freedom. They are taking all your rights, your very individuality; they are people whose only will is for power. They have a different kind of insanity, but it seems to be very fitting. There seems to be a certain synchronicity between the insane people who want to get rid of responsibility without knowing that they are getting rid of their very soul, and the other insane people, who love only one thing, power.

I want individuals to be absolutely free, responsible, alert, aware, neither allowing anybody to dictate to them nor allowing themselves to dictate to anybody. It has to be a beautiful communion. It is not based on any dictatorial ideology. It is based, basically, on ultimate freedom. And if freedom is the ultimate goal then it should be your first step too, because only the first step will lead you to the last step. It is not possible that your whole life you are just a beast of burden, doing things that people tell you to do and then suddenly one day you will become enlightened. That is not possible.

You will have to take all the responsibility for what you are doing. And you will have to grow in your consciousness and awareness so that only the right flows through your actions, so that whatever you do beautifies your world, helps people. Naturally, you will find it difficult, but don't be stuck to your Germanhood; that is a kind of disease. The world has suffered two world wars because of Germans. Don't be too concerned that you may go wrong. It is good to go wrong sometimes; just don't go wrong again on the same point—do something else, some new wrong. Always be in search of some novelty. Mistakes are absolutely needed for learning, but one should not commit the same mistake again.

Everybody has to be aware of it: nobody is responsible for you. And you don't have to ask anybody's permission. Even if you commit something wrong there is a famous law, Steward's Law: *It is easier to be forgiven than to get permission.* And remember another law; it is dangerous, so never follow it. It is called Jacob's Law: *To err is human. To blame it on someone else is even more human.*

Don't do it, ever. To err is human, and to accept your responsibility is the dignity of a human being. Don't go on thinking about what to do—do something!

Parkinson's Law is: Delay is the deadliest form of denial. Don't delay. Do something that seems appropriate in the situation and congenial to your spirit. And it is not that you have to go on *doing* continuously. Doing is not the goal of life, *being* is the goal of life. Doing is only to support your survival so that you can find your being. So don't wait for somebody else to tell you.

But throughout all these centuries that man has passed through, this has been the case—always looking to the politicians, looking to the priest, looking to neurotic people who proclaim themselves prophets, the son of God, messengers of God. People who don't want to take any responsibility immediately fall into their trap. And all your prophets and all your messengers of God are so ordinary! Your holy scriptures are not even worthy to be called great literature; it is third-rate journalism, not much more. And they are bringing laws and rules and regulations for you, and people have accepted all kinds of nonsense just in order not to seek and search for themselves.

To avoid search, to avoid seeking, people have even avoided thinking—somebody should do the job for them! The people who have been giving you your moral codes, your ethics, your life styles, are the people who remind me of another law, Maud's Law: *A conclusion is the place where you get tired of thinking.* All the conclusions that your prophets have given to you are nothing but where they got tired of thinking.

Just the other night, I was looking at a beautiful story. I became interested because it was saying why Moses and all his Jews, his followers, went on wandering in the desert for forty years. So I became interested, because it seemed the man was going to give some idea why. The idea suggested was that they had lost a quarter, so they looked all over the desert; it took forty years. Nobody knows whether they found the quarter or not; I don't think so.

The people you have been following are great people, great in their neuroses. This rule will explain it to you. Woop's Rule for Drinking—they have given you ideas for everything: *I always drink standing up because it is much easier to sit down when I get drunk standing up, than it is to get standing up when I get drunk sitting down.*

Avoid these thinkers. They have dictated to humanity for long enough. Now, stand up on your own two legs. Remember that you are alone, there is no God, there are no messengers, and there is no dictator. You have to be decisive about your own life. It is your life and you have to live it according to your own style. Only then you can make your life a celebration; otherwise it is burdened with so many rules and regulations that you cannot dance with that much burden.

I think a few jokes may do for you. My only fear is that you are a German, so whether you will get them or not is uncertain. They say that when you tell a joke to an Englishman, he laughs twice; once just to be polite, and then in the middle of the night when he gets it. A German laughs only once, because everybody else is laughing. And if you tell a joke to a Jew, he will not laugh at all. On the contrary, he will say to you that it is an old joke and, moreover, you are telling it all wrong.

But I think being around me for so long, you may have started getting, if not the whole joke, something of it...!

> A priest and a drunken bus driver arrived at the pearly gates where they met St. Peter. "I am the village priest and would like to be admitted to heaven," said the priest.
>
> "And I am the village bus driver and I want to come in too," said the drunk.
>
> "Okay," said St. Peter. "You, Mr. Priest, will have to wait over there for a few years, but you Mr. Bus Driver, you can go right in."
>
> "But wait a minute," said the priest, "I preached every Sunday in church and taught people how to pray and be good. He is nothing but a drunkard."
>
> "Listen," said St. Peter, "when you preached everybody slept. But when he drove, everybody prayed like crazy."

Six

Freedom Is Not License

Osho,

Is man responsible enough to have freedom without control?

Control is a dirty word. It has not four letters in it, but it is a four-letter word.

And when I talk about freedom I don't mean license. You may understand it that way. When I say freedom you may understand license, because that's how things go. A controlled mind, whenever it hears about freedom immediately understands it as license. License is the opposite pole of control. Freedom is just in between, just exactly in the middle, where there is no control and no license. Freedom has its own discipline, but it is not enforced by any authority. It comes out of your awareness, out of authenticity. Freedom should never be misunderstood as license; otherwise you will again miss.

Awareness brings freedom. In freedom there is no need for control, because there is no possibility for license. It is because of license that you have been forced to control, and if you remain licentious the society will go on controlling you. It is because of your licentiousness that the policeman exists, and the judge and the politician and the courts, and they go on forcing you to control yourself. And in controlling yourself you miss the whole point of being alive, because you miss celebration. How can you celebrate if you are too controlled?

55

It happens almost every day. When people come to see me who are very much controlled and disciplined, it is almost impossible to penetrate their skulls; they are too thick, they have walls of stone around them. They have become stony, they have become ice cold, the warmth is lost. Because if you are warm, there is fear—you may do something. So they have killed themselves, completely poisoned themselves. To remain in control, they have found only one solution and that is not to live at all. Be a stone buddha; then you will be able to pretend that you are patient, silent, disciplined.

But that is not what I am teaching here. Control has to be dropped as much as license. Now you will be puzzled. You can choose either control or license. You say, "If I drop control, I will become licentious. If I drop license then I have to become controlled." But I tell you, if you become aware, control and license both go down the same drain. They are two aspects of the same coin, and in awareness they are not needed.

It happened:

> An eighteen year-old boy, who had always been somewhat shy and retiring, one evening decided to change himself. He came down from his bedroom, all slicked up, and snapped at his father, "Look, I'm going out on the town—I'm going to find some beautiful girls. I'm going to get blind drunk and have a great time. I'm going to do all the things a fellow of my age should be doing in the prime of life and get a bit of adventure and excitement, so just don't try and stop me!"
>
> His old man said, "Try and stop you? Hold on, son, I'm coming with you!"

All controlled people are in that state, bubbling inside and ready to explode into licentiousness. Go and see your monks in the monasteries. In India we have that type of neurosis very much. They are all neurotics. This is something to be understood: either you become erotic or you become neurotic. If you repress your eros, your eroticness, you become neurotic. If you drop your neurosis, you become erotic. And both are types of madness. One should be simply oneself—neither neurotic nor erotic, available to all situations, ready to face whatsoever life brings, ready to accept and live, but always alert, conscious, aware, mindful.

So the only thing to be constantly remembered is self-remembrance. You should not forget yourself. Always move from the innermost core of your being. Let actions flow from there, from your very center of being, and whatsoever you do will be virtuous.

Virtue is a function of awareness.

If you do something from the periphery, it may not look like a sin, but it is sin. The society may be happy with you, but you cannot be happy with yourself. The society may praise you, but deep down you will go on condemning yourself because you will know you have missed life—and missed for nothing. What is the praise of the society? If people call you a saint, what is it? Nothing but gossip. How does it matter? You have missed godliness for gossip. You have missed life for these foolish people who are all around, for their good opinion.

Live life from your very center. This is all that meditation is about. By and by, you will come to feel a discipline that is not forced, not cultivated, which arises spontaneously, arises naturally like a flower blooms. Then you will have the whole of life available, and you will have your whole being available. And when your whole being and the whole of life meet, between the two arises that which is godliness, between the two arises that which is nirvana.

Seven

Consciousness Evolving Means Society Dissolving

Social rules seem to be a basic need for human beings. Yet, no society has ever helped man to realize himself. Can you please explain what kind of relationship exists between individuals and society, and how they can help each other to evolve?

It is a very complex question, but very fundamental too. In the whole existence, only man needs rules. No other animal needs any rules.

The first thing that has to be understood is that there is something artificial about rules. The reason man needs them is that he has left being an animal and he has not yet become human; he is in a limbo. That is the need for all the rules. If he were an animal, there would be no need. Animals live perfectly well without any rules, constitutions, laws, courts. If man really becomes human, not only in name but in reality...

Very few people have realized that up to now; for example, for men like Socrates, Zarathustra, Bodhidharma, there is no need of any rules. They are alert enough not to do any harm to anybody. There is no need for any laws, for any constitutions. If the whole society evolves to be authentically human, there will be love but there will not be law.

The problem is that man needed rules, laws, governments, courts, armies, police forces, because he lost his natural behavior of being an animal, and he has not gained another natural status again. He is just in between. He is nowhere, he is a chaos. To control that chaos all these things are needed. The problem becomes more complex because these forces that were evolved to control man—religions, states, courts—became so powerful. They had to be given power; otherwise how would they control people? So we fell into a slavery on our own. Now that they have become powerful, they don't want to drop their vested interests. They don't want man to evolve.

You are asking me how man and the society, the individual and the society, can evolve. You do not understand the problem at all. If the individual evolves, society dissolves. The society exists only because the individual is not allowed to evolve. All these powers have for centuries been controlling man, and enjoying their power, their prestige. They are not ready to let man evolve, to let man grow to a point where they become useless.

There are many situations that will help you to understand. It happened in China, twenty-five centuries ago:

Lao Tzu became very famous, a wise man, and he was without any doubt one of the wisest men ever. The emperor of China asked him very humbly to become his chief of the supreme court, because nobody could guide the country's laws better than him. He tried to persuade the emperor, "I am not the right man," but the emperor was insisting.

Lao Tzu said, "If you don't listen to me, you will be convinced that I am not the right man after just one day in the court—because the system is wrong. Out of humbleness I was not saying the truth to you. Either I can exist, or your law and your order and your society can exist. So let us try it."

The first day, a thief was brought into the court who had stolen almost half the treasures of the richest man in the capital. Lao Tzu listened to the case and then he said that the thief and the richest man should both go to jail for six months. The rich man said, "What are you saying? I have been stolen from, I have been robbed—what kind of justice is this, that you are sending me to jail for the same time as the thief?"

Lao Tzu said, "I am certainly being unfair to the thief. Your need to be in jail is greater, because you have collected so much money, deprived so many people of money that thousands of people are poor and downtrodden. And you are collecting and collecting money—for what? Your very greed is creating these thieves. You are responsible. The primary crime is yours."

Lao Tzu's logic is absolutely clear. If there are going to be too many poor people and only a few rich people, you cannot stop thieves; you cannot stop stealing. The only way to stop it is to have a society where everybody has enough to fulfill his needs, and nobody has unnecessary accumulation just out of greed.

The rich man said, "Before you send me to jail I want to see the emperor, because this is not according to the constitution; this is not according to the law of the country."

Lao Tzu said, "That is the fault of the constitution and the fault of the law of the country. I am not responsible for it. You can see the emperor."

So the rich man said to the emperor, "Listen, this man should be immediately deposed from his post; he is dangerous. Today I am going into jail, tomorrow *you* will be in jail! If you want to save yourself, this man has to be thrown out; he is absolutely dangerous. And he is very rational, what he is saying is right, I can understand it. But he will destroy us."

The king understood it perfectly well. "If this rich man is a criminal, then I am the greatest criminal in the country. Lao Tzu will not hesitate to send me to jail."

Lao Tzu was relieved of his post. He said, "I told you before, you were unnecessarily wasting my time. I was saying I am not the right man. The reality is, your society, your law, your constitution are not the right constitution, not the right law. You need wrong people to run this whole wrong system."

The problem is that the forces we created to keep man from falling apart into chaos are now so powerful that they don't want to leave you free to grow—because if you are capable of growing, becoming an individual, alert, aware and conscious, there will be no need of all these people. They will lose all their jobs, and with their jobs, their prestige, their power, their leadership, their priesthood, their popehood—everything will be gone. So now those who were needed for protection in the beginning, have turned into the enemies of humanity.

My approach is not to fight against these people—they are powerful, they have armies, they have money, they have everything. You cannot fight with them, you will be destroyed. The only way out of this mess is to silently start growing your own consciousness, which they cannot prevent by any force. In fact they cannot even know what is going on inside you.

I offer you the alchemy of inner transformation. Change your inner being. And the moment you are changed, completely transformed, you will suddenly see you are out of the imprisonment, you are no longer a slave. You were a slave because of your chaos.

It happened in the Russian revolution: The day the revolution succeeded, one woman started walking in Moscow in the middle of the road. The policeman said, "This is not right. You cannot walk in the middle of the road."

The woman said, "But now we are free!"

Even if you are free, you will have to follow the rules of traffic; otherwise traffic will become impossible. If cars and people are running everywhere they want, turning wherever they want, don't take any note of the lights, people will be simply getting into accidents, being killed. This will bring the army in, to enforce the law that you have to walk to the right or to the left, whichever is chosen by the country—but nobody can walk in the middle. Then, at the point of a gun, you will have to follow. I always remember that woman; she is very symbolic.

Freedom does not mean chaos. Freedom means more responsibility, so much responsibility that nobody need interfere in your life. It means that you can be left alone, that the government need not interfere with you, that the police need not interfere with you, that the law has nothing to do with you—you are simply out of their world.

This is my approach if you really want to transform humanity: each individual should start growing on his own.

And in fact, a crowd is not needed for growth. Growth is something like a child growing in a mother's womb: no crowd is needed; the mother has just to be careful.

A new man has to be born in you. You have to become the womb of a new man. Nobody will come to know about it, and it is better that nobody knows about it. You simply go on doing your ordinary work, living in the ordinary world, being simple and ordinary—not becoming revolutionaries, reactionaries, punks and skinheads. That is not going to help. That is sheer stupidity. It is out of frustration, but still it is insane. The society is insane, and out of frustration you become insane. The society is not afraid of these people; the society is afraid only of people who can become so centered, so conscious that laws become useless for them. They always do right. They are beyond the grip of the so-called powerful interests.

If individuals grow, society will diminish. The way they have known society, with the government, with the army, with the courts, with the policemen, with the jails—this society will diminish.

Certainly, because there are so many human beings, new forms of collectivities will come into being. I would not like to call them society, just to avoid the confusion between the words. I call the new collectivity a *commune*. The word is significant: it means a place where people are not only living together, but where people are in deep communion.

To live together is one thing; we are doing it: in every city, every town, thousands of people are living together—but what togetherness is there? People don't even know their neighbors. They live in the same skyscraper, thousands of people, and they never come to know that they are living in the same house. It is not togetherness, because there is no communion. It is simply a crowd, not a community. So I would like to replace the word *society* with the word *commune*.

Society has existed on certain basic principles. You will have to remove them, otherwise the society will not disappear. The first and the most important unit of society has been the family: if the family remains the way it is, then the society cannot disappear, then the church cannot disappear, then religions cannot disappear. Then we cannot create one world, one humanity.

The family is psychologically out of date. It is not that the family has always been there; there was a time when there was no family, people lived in tribes. The family came into existence because of private property. There were powerful people who managed to have more private property than anybody else, and they wanted it to be given to their children. Up to then there was no question...men and women were meeting out of love; there was no marriage and no family. But once property came into existence, the man became very possessive of the woman. He turned the woman also into part of his property.

In Indian languages the woman is called *property*. In China the woman became so much a property that even if a husband killed his wife there was no law against it, no crime was committed. You are absolutely free to destroy your property—you can burn your furniture, you can burn your house. It is not a crime, it is your house. You can kill your wife.... With private property, the woman also became private property, and every strategy was used so that the man could be absolutely certain that the child that was born from his wife was really his own. Now, this is a difficult problem: the father can never be absolutely certain; only the mother knows. But the father created every kind of barrier for the movement of the woman so that she could not come into contact with other men. All possibilities and all doors are closed.

It is not a coincidence that only old women go into your churches and temples, because that is the only place they were allowed to go. It is known perfectly well that the church is defensive of the family. The church knows that once the family is gone, the church is gone. And the church, of course, is the last place where some romantic affair can happen. They have taken every precaution: the priest has to be celibate. These are guarantees—that the priest is celibate, he is against sex, he is against women—in different religions, in different ways.

The Jaina monk cannot touch a woman; in fact the woman should not come closer than eight feet to the Jaina monk. The Buddhist monk is not allowed to touch a woman. There are religions which don't allow women to enter into their religious places, or they have separating partitions: men have the main part, the women have a small corner—but separated. The men cannot even see them; meeting is impossible. Many religions, like Mohammedanism, have covered their women's faces. Mohammedan women's faces have become pale because they never see the sunlight. Their whole body is covered; their face is covered. In every possible way... The woman is not to be educated, because education gives people strange kinds of thoughts. People start thinking, people start arguing....

The woman was not allowed to have any paid career, because that means independence. So she was cut off, excluded from every nook and corner, just for this simple reason: so that you are certain that your son is really your son. Those who were really powerful, for example kings, had male servants castrated, because they were moving in the palace, working, serving. They had to be castrated; otherwise, there was a danger... And there was danger because every emperor had hundreds of wives, many of whom he would never see. Naturally, those women could fall in love with anybody...but only castrated men were allowed into the palace, so even if they fell in love they could not create children. That was the basic thing.

The family has to disappear and give place to the commune. A commune means that we have pooled all our energies, all our money, everything into a single pool—which will be taking care of all the people. The children will belong to the commune, so there is no question of individual heritage. And it is so economical... I have seen in my commune in America, five thousand people were there—that means two thousand five hundred kitchens would have been needed if they were living separately. But there was only one kitchen for five thousand people, and only fifteen people were running it. And remember, everybody is not a good cook! Two thousand five hundred people cannot afford the best cooks separately, but a five-thousand-person commune can afford the best cooks, the best food. It can afford doctors to look into whether what they are eating is junk or food—most people are eating junk.

To be right the food has to be medically decided. In my commune fifteen people were preparing the food, doctors were looking at it, its hygiene, its cleanliness and its nutritious value. It is nutrition that should be valued. Flavor is a small thing; that can be given to any kind of food, good flavor. You need not eat junk just for flavor—and if you eat junk, sooner or later you are going to become junk. There are so many junkies all around! If you look in their heads you will find ice cream, nothing else...spaghetti!

You need a very proportionate, calculated food balance to keep all your needs completely fulfilled, food that helps consciousness to grow, food that makes you more loving, more peaceful, food that destroys your anger, your hatred. It is your chemistry that food changes, and all these things—anger, hatred, love, compassion—are connected with your chemistry. There should be a chemist to look at what kind of food is being given to people. If you pool all your energies, all your money and all your resources, every commune can be rich and every commune can enjoy being alive equally.

Once individuals are growing and communes are growing side by side, society will disappear, and with society all the evils that the society has created.

I will give you one example. Only in China was a tremendously revolutionary step taken two thousand years ago. This was that the doctor had to be paid by the patient while the patient remained healthy; if he fell sick, then the doctor was not to be paid. That looks very strange. We pay the doctor when we are sick, and he makes us healthy again. But this is dangerous, because you are making the doctor dependent on your sickness. Sickness becomes his interest: the more people fall sick, the more he can earn. His interest becomes not health, but sickness. If everybody remains healthy, then the doctor will be the only one who will be sick!

They made a revolutionary idea, practical, that every person has a physician, and while the person remains healthy the doctor is paid every month. It is the duty of the doctor to keep people healthy—and naturally he will keep people healthy because he is being paid for it. If a person falls sick, the doctor loses money. When there are epidemics the doctor goes bankrupt. Right now it is just the opposite. The doctor gets rich when there is an epidemic.

But this is a very wrong system. The commune should pay the doctor to keep the commune healthy, and if anybody gets sick the doctor's salary is cut. So health is the business of the doctor, not sickness. And you can see the difference: in the West, the doctor's business is called *medicine*, which relates to sickness. In the East it is called *ayurveda*, which means the science of life—not of sickness. The basic business of the doctor should be that people should live long, should live healthy, whole, and he should be paid for it. So each commune can afford very easily to keep the doctor, the plumber, the engineer—whatever is needed. That is the commune's responsibility to take care of, and the people who serve the commune should be rotating so there is no concentration of power arising again.

The committee of the commune should be in rotation; every year new people are coming in and old people are going out, so nobody becomes addicted to power. Power is the worst drug that people can become addicted to; it should be given, but in very small doses and not for a long time. Let the individual grow and let the commune grow—and forget all about society; don't fight with it. Don't even say, "We are creating an alternative society."

We have nothing to do with society; let society go on as it is. If it wants to live it will have to change its mode, its form, its structure, and it will have to become a commune. If it wants to die, let it die. There is no harm. The world is overpopulated; it needs only one-fourth of its population. So the old rotten heads who cannot conceive of anything new, who are absolutely blind and cannot see that what they are doing is harmful and poisonous... if they have decided to die, then let them die silently. Don't disturb them.

I don't teach you to be revolutionaries. I want you to be very silent, almost underground transformers. Because all the revolutions have failed... now the only possible way is that we should do it so silently and so peacefully that it can happen.

There are things which happen only in silence. For example, if you love roses, you should not pull up the rosebush every day to look at its roots; otherwise you will kill it. Those roots have to remain hidden. Silently they go on doing their work.

My people have to be just like roots: silently go on doing the work, changing yourself, changing anybody who is interested; spreading the methods that can change; creating small pools, small groups, small communes and, wherever possible, bigger communes. But let this whole thing happen very silently, without creating any upheaval.

The individual can exist only if society dies; they cannot coexist. It is time for the society to be dead, and we will find new ways of togetherness which will not be formal, which will be more of the heart. The family prevents it, the family draws a boundary around every child. It says, "I am your father, so love me. I am your mother, so love me. This is your family. If there is need, sacrifice yourself for the family."

The same idea is projected on a bigger scale as nation: "This is your nation. If it needs you, sacrifice yourself." Society, family, nation... it is the same idea becoming bigger and bigger. So my basic attack is on the family. The family is the root cause of all our problems. Our poverty, our sickness, our madness, our emptiness, our lovelessness—the family is the cause. And the family is the cause of all our conditionings, from the very beginning. It starts conditioning your mind: you are a Jew, you are a Christian, you are a Hindu, you are this and you are that—and the poor child does not know what nonsense you are talking about.

The family gives you as inheritance the whole past and the load, the burden of all those things that have been proved wrong for hundreds of years. You are loaded with all those wrong things, and your mind is closed and clogged and it cannot receive anything new that goes against it. Your mind is simply full of wrong things.

If the children are in the hands of the commune... I have experimented and found it immensely successful. The children are far happier because they are far freer. No conditioning is stamped on them; they mature earlier, because nobody is trying to make them dependent so they become independent. Nobody is going out of their way to help them, so they have to learn how to help themselves. This brings maturity, clarity, a certain strength. And they are all meditating: meditation is not a conditioning; it is simply sitting silently, doing nothing, just enjoying the silence—the silence of the night, the silence of the early morning... and slowly, slowly you become acquainted with the silence that pervades your inner being. Then the moment you close your eyes you fall into the pool of a silent lake, which is fathomless. And out of that silence you are rejuvenated every moment.

Out of that silence comes your love, comes your beauty, comes a special depth to your eyes; a special aura to your being, a strength to your individuality, and a self-respect.

Individual freedom and authority on one side, and authoritarianism and dictatorship on the other side, move man's life and his aspirations. Please comment on this.

It is the same problem, the same question, phrased differently. Society is authoritarian; the church is authoritarian; the educational system is authoritarian. They all say, "Whatever we say is right, and you need not question it. You have simply to follow."

And there are problems, for example, in the educational system. I have been a student, I have been a professor, and I know that for the best part of life a person is being ruined by authoritarian people in the schools, in the colleges, in the universities. I was expelled from many colleges for the simple reason that I could not accept any authoritarianism. I said, "You prove it and I am ready to accept it. But without proving it, without giving right arguments for it, without making it a rational statement, I am not going to accept it."

And I was fighting in every subject, because in every subject the teachers were simply lecturing. Students were taking notes, because all that was needed was to repeat in the examination papers what the teachers had been telling them. And the better you repeat, exactly like a parrot, the more credit you get.

Small things they were in difficulty to prove, and it became embarrassing to them. Every day it was a question; anything they would say, I would stand up immediately— and I was asking relevant questions—"On what grounds...?"

For example, one of the professors who was teaching religions made the statement that the Vedas, the Hindu holy scriptures, were written by God. I had to stand up. I said, "I object. In the first place you have not been able to prove the existence of God. In the second place, now you are saying that these books, which are full of rubbish, are written by God. Have you ever looked into the Vedas?" I asked him, "Have you ever read from the first page to the last page?" There are four Vedas, big volumes. "I have brought all four volumes with me, and at random I can open and read and let the whole class decide whether this is a statement God could have written."

The Vedas are full of prayers. Now, God cannot pray; to whom will he be praying? And prayers for such stupid things that it is simply ridiculous to say that they are written by God. One Brahmin is praying, "I have been continuously doing all the rituals, living according to the scriptures and you have still not given me a child. Give me a child; that will be a proof that my prayers have been heard."

I asked him, "How could God have written this passage? It is written by someone and addressed to God, but it cannot be written by God himself. And if this is the situation of God, then that poor fellow should not be bothered about it. God is asking about a child from somebody else, so why should we not ask from the same source? Why should we bother this poor fellow?"

Their only answer, finally, was that every college would reject me. The principal would say, "We are sorry. We know you are right, but we have to run the college. You will destroy the whole institution. Professors are threatening to resign, students are saying that you don't allow the professors to teach because on a single point every day the whole period is lost. Eight months have passed, and the course will not be finished in the coming two months if the same thing continues. The students have come here to pass examinations; they are not interested in truth, they are not interested in the validity of any statement. Their only reason to be here is to get a certificate. And you are a strange fellow—you don't seem to be interested in certificates."

I said, "I am not interested at all in certificates. What will I do with certificates from these people who don't know anything? I cannot think of these people as my examiners. The day you give me the certificate, I will tear it up immediately in front of you—because these people can't answer any real questions."

But the whole system is geared in that way. When I became a professor myself, I had to make a new arrangement. The arrangement was that in each forty-minute period, twenty minutes I would teach the syllabus as it is written in the books, and twenty minutes I would criticize it. My students said, "We will go mad."

I said, "That is your problem—but I cannot leave these statements without criticism. You can choose; when your examination comes you can choose to write whichever you want. If you want to fail, choose my part. If you want to pass, choose the first part. I am making it clear; I am not deceiving anybody. And I cannot go on deceiving you by teaching you something I think is absolutely wrong."

The vice-chancellor finally had to call me, and he said to me, "This is a strange type of teaching. I have been receiving every day reports that half the time you teach the syllabus and half the time you have your arguments, which destroy the whole thing that you have taught them. So they come as empty as they had gone in... in fact, in more of a mess!"

I said, "I'm not worried about anybody. What have they done with me all these years when I was a student? I was expelled from one college and then another. And you can come one day and listen to whether I am doing any injustice to the prescribed course. When I teach the prescribed course, I do it as totally as possible, to make it clear."

He came one day and he listened, and after twenty minutes he said, "That is really great. I had been also a student of philosophy, but nobody has ever told me this way."

I said, "This is only half the talk. You just wait, because now I am going to destroy it completely, step by step."

And when I destroyed it completely he said, "My God! Now I can understand what the poor students are reporting to me. You are not supposed to be a professor in this structure of education. I can understand that what you are doing is absolutely honest, but this system does not create people of intelligence; this system only creates people of good memory—and that's what is needed. We need clerks, we need stationmasters, we need postmasters—and these students don't need intelligence, they need a good memory."

I said, "In other words you need computers, not people. If this is your educational system, then sooner or later you are going to replace human beings with computers"—and that's what they are doing. Everywhere they are replacing important positions with computers, because computers are more reliable; they are just memory, no intelligence.

Man, however repressed, has a certain intelligence. The man who dropped atom bombs on Hiroshima and Nagasaki—if it had been a computer, there was no question: at the exact time, at the exact mileage, it would have dropped the bomb and returned. It would have been simply mechanical. But the man who was dropping the bomb, howsoever you may have destroyed his intelligence, had to think twice about what he was doing. Killing one hundred thousand people who were absolutely innocent, who were civilians, who were not army people, who had not done any harm to anybody—is it right?

Now everywhere, all nuclear weapons are in the hands of computers, not in the hands of human beings. Computers will fight the third world war. Human beings will be killed, that is another matter. Computers don't care whether humanity survives or disappears; it does not matter to them, but they will do exact and efficient work that man cannot do. Man may hesitate in destroying the whole of humanity; something of intelligence, just a little bit of intelligence is enough to create the question, "What am I doing?"

All our institutions, our religions are authoritarian. They don't tell you why: "Just do it because it is written in the book, because Jesus says so." Jesus has not given a single argument why it should be done; he has not given a single rational ground for any of his doctrines. Neither has Moses done that, nor has Krishna. Krishna simply says to Arjuna, "This is from God: You have to fight." This is authoritarianism. And God is used, manipulated in every situation, to make whatever you are saying absolutely unquestionable.

We have to destroy all authoritarianism in the world.

Authority is totally different. Authoritarianism is connected with the society, with the church; authority is something which is concerned with the individual realization. If I say something to you, I say it with authority. This simply means I am saying it because this is my experience—but it does not mean that you have to believe it. It is enough that you listened to it; now you can think over it, you can decide for or against.

To me, what is important is not that you decide for; what is important to me is that you decide on your own. It may be against it, it does not matter—but the decision should come from your own being. If it doesn't come from your own being, then you are making me authoritarian.

I am speaking from my authority. Please don't make me into an authoritarian, because I am simply stating the fact with as much force and fire as I am capable of, so that it is absolutely clear to you—and now you are free to decide. I am not deciding for you, and I am not asking you to have faith in me or believe in me. I am simply asking, "Give me a little chance, think about what I am saying to you, and I will be grateful that you thought about it." That's enough. Your thinking will give you a sharper intelligence, and I trust in intelligence. If you think, and your intelligence becomes sharper, I know that whatever you conclude will be right.

And even if you conclude wrong one time, it does not matter. One has to fall many times and rise up again. That's how life is. One has to commit mistakes and learn from them, and change every stumbling block into a steppingstone.

But around me there is no question of any belief or faith. With individual freedom, authoritarianism dies and a new thing arises: authority. Each individual is capable of having experiences of his own; then he has authority, then he can say, "I have seen it, I have tasted it. I have enjoyed it, I have danced it. And it is not a question that I am quoting from some scripture, I am simply opening my heart to you."

Authority belongs to experience.

Authoritarianism belongs to somebody else, not to you; hence it creates slavery, not freedom. And to me, freedom is the ultimate value, because only in freedom can you blossom, and can you blossom to your fullest possibility.

Is society a real fact determined by the existence of man, or is it a false concept, a conditioning which exists only because man is asleep?

Society is not an existential reality. It is created by man because man is asleep, because man is in a chaos, because man is not capable of having freedom without turning it into licentiousness. Man is not capable of having freedom and not taking advantage of it. So it is an artificial, but necessary, creation of man.

Because society is artificial, it can be dissolved. Because it was necessary once, it does not mean it has to be necessary forever. Man just has to change those conditions which made it necessary. And it is good that it is not existential, otherwise there would be no way to get rid of it.

It is our own manufactured thing. We can destroy it any day we want.

How to evolve out of the collectivity of nations without falling into the barbarity of single egos fighting against each other?

All your questions are centered on one thing. I would like to give you one answer.

I am reminded of a parable....

A great master was sitting on the seashore, on the beach, and a man who was seeking for truth came to him, touched his feet and asked, "If I am not disturbing you, I would like to do anything that you suggest which can help me to find the truth."

The master simply closed his eyes and remained silent.

The man shook his head. He said in his own mind, "This man seems to be crazy. I am asking him a question and he is closing his eyes." He shook the man and said, "What about my question?"

The master said, "I answered it. Just sit silently...don't do anything, and the grass grows by itself. You need not bother about it—everything will happen. You just sit silently, enjoy silence."

The man said, "Can you give it a name—because people will be asking me, 'What are you doing?'"

So the master wrote on the sand with his finger: meditation.

The man said, "This is too small an answer. Be a little more elaborate."

The master wrote in big letters: MEDITATION.

The man said, "But these are simply big letters. You are writing the same thing."

The old master said, "If I say more than that, then it will be wrong. If you can understand, then just do what I have told you, and you will know."

And that's my answer too.

Each individual has to become a meditator, a silent watcher, so that he can discover himself. This discovery is going to change everything around him. And if we can change many people through meditation, we can create a new world.

Many people have been hoping for centuries for a new world, but they had no idea how to create it. I am giving you the exact science how to create it. Meditation is the name of that science.

Eight

Terrorism – Your Inner Volcano of Violence

Osho,

Is the rise of terrorism over the last decade in some way symbolic of what is happening to society in general?

Everything is deeply related with everything else that happens. The phenomenon of terrorism is certainly related with what is happening in the society. The society is falling apart. Its old order, discipline, morality, religion, everything has been found to be wrongly based. It has lost its power over people's conscience.

Terrorism simply symbolizes that to destroy human beings does not matter, that there is nothing in human beings which is indestructible, that it is all matter—and you cannot kill matter, you can only change its form. Once man is taken to be only a combination of matter, and no place is given for a spiritual being inside him, then to kill becomes just play.

The nations are irrelevant because of nuclear weapons. If the whole world can be destroyed together within minutes, the alternative can only be that the whole world should be together. Now it cannot remain divided; its division is dangerous, because division can become war any moment. The division cannot be tolerated. Only one war is enough to destroy everything, and there is not much time left for man to understand that we should create a world where the very possibility of war does not exist.

Terrorism has many undercurrents. One is that because of nuclear weapons, the nations are pouring their energy into that field, thinking that the old weapons are out of date. They are out of date, but individuals can start using them. And you cannot use nuclear weapons against individuals—that would be simply stupid. One individual terrorist throws a bomb, it does not justify that a nuclear missile should be sent.

What I want to emphasize is that the nuclear weapon has given individual people a certain freedom to use old weapons, a freedom which was not possible in the old days because the governments were also using the same weapons.

Now the governments are concentrated on destroying the old weapons, throwing them in the ocean, selling them to countries that are poor and cannot afford nuclear weapons. And all those terrorists are coming from these poor countries, with the same weapons that have been sold to their countries. And they have a strange protection: you cannot use nuclear weapons against them, you cannot throw atom bombs at them.

They can throw bombs at you, and you are suddenly impotent. You have a vast amount of atomic bombs, nuclear bombs in your hands—but sometimes where a needle is useful, a sword may not be of any use. You may have the sword; that does not mean that you are necessarily in a superior position to the man who has a needle, because there are situations in which only the needle will work, the sword will not be of any use.

Those small weapons from the old times were piling up, and the big powers had to dispose of them. You could drown them in the ocean, but that meant so much money, so much manpower, so much energy had gone to waste; economically it was disastrous. But just to go on piling them up was also economically impossible. How many weapons can you gather? There is a limit. And when you get a new way of killing people more efficiently, then the old simply has to be got rid of. So it was thought that it would be better to sell them to poor countries. Poor countries cannot create nuclear weapons, it costs too much. And these weapons were coming cheap, as "help," so they accepted it. But these weapons cannot be used in a war; in a war these weapons were already useless. But nobody had seen the possibility that these weapons could be used individually, and a new phenomenon, terrorism, can come out of it.

Now, a terrorist has a strange power, even over the greatest powers. He can throw bombs at the White House without any fear, because what you have is too big and you cannot throw it at him. And these are the weapons sold by you! But the phenomenon was not conceived of, because human psychology is not understood.

My understanding is that the way he has lived, man needs a war every ten to twelve years. He accumulates so much anger, so much rage, so much violence, that nothing short of a war will give him release. So, war after war, there is a gap of only ten to fifteen years. That gap is a kind of relaxation. But again you start accumulating, because the same psychology is working—the same jealousy, the same violence.

And man is basically a hunter; he is not by nature vegetarian. First he became a hunter, and for thousands of years he was just a meat-eater, and cannibalism was prevalent everywhere. To eat human beings caught from the opposing tribe you were fighting with was perfectly ethical. All that history is carried in the unconscious of humanity.

Religions have imposed things on man very superficially; his unconscious is not in agreement. Every man is living in a disagreement with himself. So whenever he can find a chance…for a beautiful cause, freedom, democracy, socialism, any beautiful word can become an umbrella to hide his ugly unconscious, which simply wants to destroy and enjoys destruction.

Now a world war has become almost impossible; otherwise there would have been no terrorism. Enough time has passed since the second world war; the third world war should have happened near about 1960. It has not happened. This has been the routine for the whole of history, and man is programmed for it.

It has been observed by psychologists that in wartime people are more happy than in peacetime. In wartime their life has a thrill; in peacetime they look bored. In wartime, early in the morning they are searching for the newspaper, listening to the radio. Things may be happening far away, but they are excited. Something in them feels an affinity. A war that should have happened somewhere between 1955 and 1960 has not happened, and man is burdened with the desire to kill, with the desire to destroy. It is just that he wants good names for it.

Terrorism is going to become bigger and bigger, because the third world war is almost impossible. And the stupid politicians have no other alternative. Terrorism simply means that what was being done on a social scale now has to be done individually. It will grow. It can only be prevented if we change the very base of human understanding—which is a Himalayan task; more so because these same people whom you want to change will fight you; they won't allow you to change them easily. In fact they love bloodshed; they don't have the courage to say so.

Until we change the basic ground of humanity, terrorism is going to become more and more a normal, everyday affair. It will happen in the airplanes, it will happen in the buses. It will start happening in the cars. It will start happening to strangers. Somebody will suddenly come and shoot you— not that you have done anything to him, but it is just that the hunter is back. The hunter was satisfied in the war. Now the war has stopped, and perhaps there is no possibility for it. The hunter is back; now we cannot fight collectively. Each individual has to do something to release his own steam.

Things are interconnected. The first thing that has to be changed is that man should be made more rejoicing— which all the religions have killed. The real criminals are not caught. These are the victims, the terrorists and other criminals. It is all the religions who are the real criminals, because they have destroyed all possibilities of rejoicing. They have destroyed the possibility of enjoying small things of life; they have condemned everything that nature provides you to make you happy, to make you feel excited, feel pleasant. They have taken everything away; and if they have not been able to take a few things away because they are so ingrained in your biology—like sex—they have at least been able to poison them.

Friedrich Nietzsche, according to me, is one of the greatest seers of the Western world; his eyes really go penetrating to the very root of a problem. But because others could not see it—their eyes were not so penetrating, nor was their intelligence so sharp—the man lived alone, abandoned, isolated, unloved, unrespected. He says in one of his statements that man has been taught by religions to condemn sex, to renounce sex. Religion has not been able to manage it; and man has tried hard but has failed, because it is so deeply rooted in his biology—it constitutes his whole body. He is born out of sex, how can he get rid of it except by committing suicide? So man has tried, and religions have helped him to get rid of it—thousands of disciplines and strategies have been used. The total result is that sex is there, but poisoned. That word *poisoned* is a tremendous insight. Religions have not been able to take it away, but they have been certainly successful in poisoning it. And the same is the situation about other things: religions condemn your living in comfort. Now, a man who is living in comfort and luxury cannot become a terrorist. Religions have condemned riches, praised poverty; now, a man who is rich cannot be a terrorist. Only the "blessed ones" who are poor can be terrorists because they have nothing to lose, and they are boiling up against the whole of society because others have things they don't have.

Religions have been trying to console them. But then came communism, a materialist religion, which provoked people and said to them, "Your old religions are all opium to the people, and it is not because of your evil actions in this life or in past lives that you are suffering poverty. It is because of the evil exploitation of the bourgeois, the super-rich that you are suffering."

The last sentence in Karl Marx's *Communist Manifesto* is: Proletariat of the whole world unite; you have nothing to lose and you have the whole world to gain. You are already poor, hungry, naked, so what can you lose? Your death will not make you more miserable than your life is making you. So why not take a chance and destroy those people who have taken everything away from you. And take those things back, distribute them.

What religions have somehow been consoling people with—although it was wrong and it was cunning and it was a lie, but it kept people in a state of being half asleep—communism suddenly made them aware of. That means this world is now never going to be peaceful if we don't withdraw all the rotten ideas that have been implanted in man.

The first are the religions. Their values should be removed so that man can smile again, can laugh again, can rejoice again, can be natural again. Second, what communism is saying has to be put clearly before the people—it is psychologically wrong. You are falling from one trap into another. No two people are equal; hence the idea of equality is nonsense. And if you decide to be equal then you have to accept a dictatorship of the proletariat. That means you have to lose your freedom.

First the church took away your freedom, the God took away your freedom. Now communism replaces your church, and it will take away your freedom. And without freedom you cannot rejoice.

You live in fear, not in joy. If we can clean the basement of the human mind's unconscious... and that's what my work is. It can be cleaned away.

The terrorism is not in the bombs, in your hands; the terrorism is in your unconscious.

Otherwise, this state of affairs is going to grow more bitter. And it seems all kinds of blind people have bombs in their hands and are throwing them at random.

The third world war would have released people for ten or fifteen years. But the third world war cannot happen because if it happens it won't relieve people, it will only destroy people. So individual violence will increase—it is increasing. And all your governments and all your religions will go on perpetuating the old strategies without understanding the new situation.

The new situation is that every human being needs to go through therapies, needs to understand his unconscious intentions, needs to go through meditations so that he can calm down, become cool—and look towards the world with a new perspective, of silence.

Nine

The Basic Fallacy of Revolutions

Osho,

Nine years ago I fell in love with Camus' book, **Man in Revolt,** *in which he comes to the conclusion that all attempts to abolish injustice through revolutions are bound to fail. Rather, he says, the only way is to create justice through living it.*

Is Camus' revolt just another expression of what you were calling rebellion?

Camus' book, *Man in Revolt,* has many great insights in it, but he still remains a philosopher. He preaches, but he does not practice. You are saying that in this book, "he comes to the conclusion that all attempts to abolish injustice through revolutions are bound to fail." That's a great insight.

It seems there is something intrinsic in the very mechanism of revolution that makes it bound to fail. First, the revolutionary is created by the old society against which he is revolting; his values, his ideals are not much different from the old. The only difference for him is that the right people are not in power; otherwise, everything is right. Only the right people have to be in power, the wrong people have to be removed, and the revolution will be accomplished in all dimensions of life.

This is a basic fallacy. It is not a question of the right or wrong people. The whole society has been conditioned to live in a reactionary way, not in a revolutionary way; it has been conditioned to be slaves, not masters. Hence, when a few people revolt against the power structure, to replace the old establishment with themselves, only then do they find out that what the old establishment was doing, they, too, have to do; otherwise, there will be immense chaos.

But that understanding comes too late, and slowly, they themselves turn into the same kind of people that they have thrown out—in fact, worse, because now they know the taste of power, and they also know how they have thrown out the people who were in power before them. Soon there will be a new generation coming, which will start talking about revolution because nothing has been changed. The old revolutionaries will be more alert to repress any possibility of a new revolution because they know how they threw out the old power structure, and they are not going to be thrown out in the same way. They will not allow freedom of speech, which is a basis for any revolution to happen, and they will crush every individual who does not follow their structure.

For sixty years in the Soviet Union, the communist regime proved far worse than the regime of the czars that it had revolted against. At least in the regime of czars, it was possible to create a revolution; but under a communist regime it was almost impossible. They didn't allow it from the very beginning. All publications were government owned, radio was government owned, television was government owned. In fact, in the name of communism, private property was taken over by the state. So to call the Soviet Union a communist country is not right—it was state capitalism.

In America, there are many capitalists, and their large number gives a certain feeling of movement and change, and the possibility of revolution. In the Soviet Union, there was only one communist and that was the state itself. All power, all wealth, all land, everything belonged to the state; the individual was denuded of all ownership. The educational institutions were all run by the government. You read only what the government wanted you to read, you listened only to government radio stations, and on the television you saw only what the government wanted you to see.

You cannot have another political party in opposition to the Communist Party because it is not a democracy—it is a dictatorship of the proletariat. It is just a name, "dictatorship of the proletariat"; and in the name of the proletariat, it is the Communist Party which is the dictator. It is the same small group of people who have been ruling for sixty years, and total power is in their hands.

Joseph Stalin, who established communist rule in Russia, killed at least one million people in his own land. These were the same people for whom the revolution was preached, and of these million people, most of them were revolutionaries. He had to kill them because now those revolutionaries were a risk. To let them live was dangerous because they were asking continually, "What happened to the revolution?" Only the people in power had changed, but the revolution seemed to be happening nowhere; all was the same. Instead of many capitalists, now there was only one capitalist, the state, which certainly made it immensely powerful. And there was no opposition party, there was no question of any opposition.

It is well known—there is no evidence to prove it, but there is every possibility of its being true—that as the revolution succeeded, Lenin, the leader of the revolution, and Trotsky, his second in command, his right hand, Commeneau, Zinoviev, and other great communist revolutionaries, were killed one by one. Lenin was given small doses of poison every day, under the pretext of giving him medicine. It was his wife who confessed that Stalin never allowed any other doctor except his own to take care of Lenin, and his condition went on worsening. Stalin did not want him to die immediately because, in Lenin's name, he first wanted to establish himself securely. Stalin was only the secretary of the party; his contribution to the revolution was not much, he was not a well-known figure in the nation or internationally. Lenin was the founder of the revolution, and Trotsky was the most influential leader—even Lenin was not such a charismatic leader as Trotsky was. Stalin kept Lenin alive, but at most half alive. While slowly, slowly poisoning him on the one hand, on the other hand he went on taking more and more power into his own hands. When Stalin was completely in control, Lenin was finished.

Lenin never ruled over Russia. After the revolution he was continuously sick; he was kept sick. Then Commeneau was caught, Zinoviev was assassinated, and Trotsky, who was the defense minister, escaped Russia fearing that now that Lenin was dead his number was going to be up. And you cannot conceive the inhumanity of man to man. The day Stalin's assassins reached Trotsky's house... he had already left the Soviet Union just a few hours before. They found only his dog in the house, and it seems almost unbelievable, but Stalin ordered the dog to be assassinated immediately— just a mad mind corrupted by power. And he sent professional murderers to find where Trotsky was; he had to be killed, he could not be left alive anywhere in the world. Trotsky had escaped to an unknown part of Mexico, far away from the Soviet Union, at the other end of the world. But they finally found him, and he was brutally murdered by being hit on his head repeatedly with a hammer. His whole skull was broken into pieces.

Trotsky was writing a biography of Joseph Stalin so future generations would know that just to change the people in power is not enough—Stalin had proved to be far worse than the czars. It is a big volume, almost one thousand pages, and a rare biography written by an enemy, so sincere, so truthful. When he was hit on his head from behind with a hammer, he was just finishing the biography. His blood is on the last pages of the book. The book is still kept in some museum in Mexico, his handwritten book with his blood on it.

All the other leaders who had been the great revolutionaries were killed, one after another, because these people were dangerous. They were still talking about revolution, and Stalin recognized the fact that no revolution was possible. It was good to talk about it before the revolution, but now that the responsibility has fallen on your own shoulders, you have to forget all about revolution. You have to establish yourself and your party in power with such force that nobody can destroy your power.

There is a beautiful story.... When Stalin died and Khrushchev became the prime minister, his first speech was to the highest inner circle of the Communist Party, called the Presidium. While he was speaking, he said, "Now I have to confess that Stalin was one of the greatest criminals. He knew only one thing: either you are for him or you are his enemy. And for the enemy, there is nothing other than death."

Somebody in the back of the auditorium shouted, "You have been with him for all these forty years. Why did you remain silent?" Khrushchev laughed and said, "I would like the honorable comrade to stand up, so that I can see who is raising the question."

Nobody stood up, and Khrushchev said, "Do you understand? If anybody stands, tomorrow he will be dead. After tomorrow, he will never be heard of again anywhere in the universe. I was also in a similar position."

The whole country became a concentration camp, and they used methods against human beings which had never been used by any other government or any other power. First, they would make an arrest if there was any suspicion... if a man had talked to someone against the Communist Party, against the government, or he had written a letter to someone indicating a slight difference with the Communist Party, he would be arrested immediately. For fifteen days he would be in police custody, and the police would not allow him to sleep; they would inject him so that he could not sleep, not even a wink. They would inject chemicals to disturb his mind, to erase his memory; they would create a false madness in the man. And then, after fifteen days, the man would be produced before the court. The government attorney would say, "He has been arrested because he is not in his right senses—he is insane."

Such a beautiful facade... and then the court would go through its procedures: the judge would ask the man, "What is your name?" And the man would look all around, because he has forgotten everything, his memory has been erased. And naturally, the judge has to declare him mad. He has to be sent into a madhouse where he will be killed; nobody will ever know what happened to him in the madhouse. Or people will be sent to Siberia where life is worse than death. Death is a rest... Siberia is not a place to live, it is a place to suffer.

The revolution utterly failed. And this was the greatest revolution as far as history is concerned; the greatest experiment, on the largest scale, with a profound philosophy to support it. The same happened to the French Revolution and to the Chinese Revolution. The very mechanism of revolution is such that its success is almost impossible. If you want to remain in power, you have to be violent, destructive—particularly destructive of those people who have revolutionary ideas. Those ideas were great and good against the older regime, but they are not good against the new regime in which you are powerful.

And all the promises have to be forgotten completely because they prove to be utopian. For example, the Russian revolutionaries had promised that they would dissolve marriage, but they never did it because the Communist Party saw that if marriage is dissolved... it is the basic unit of the nation. It would become impossible to keep the nation together, and they wanted their nation to dominate the whole world. They were against nationalism before the revolution, but afterwards Soviet Russia became a holy land. Now they wanted their power to become more and more spread all over the world. They were now imperialists, no longer against nationalism, although they continued to speak beautiful revolutionary language. They were very articulate; before the revolution they had learned all that language. Now they started talking about an international communism; but "international communism" was to be nothing but a Soviet imperialist state.

Before the revolution in China, Mao Zedong, the leader of the revolution, was a follower of Joseph Stalin. But once Mao came into power, there was immediately a conflict because Stalin wanted China also to be part of one communist block. That meant Mao's own lust for power had no place; China would also become one of the republics of the Soviet Union. Mao resisted it and they became enemies. China and the Soviet Union, both communist countries, became so antagonistic to one another that one can see why it is difficult to have an international government. Some nation will try, in the name of international government, to exert its own lust for power and rule over the whole world.

Camus was right that all attempts to abolish injustice through revolutions are bound to fail; and he was also right when he said, "The only way to create justice is through living it." That comes very close to my idea of the new man, the rebel: each individual living in a revolutionary way, on his own, having no power over others, because power certainly corrupts. But the difference is that Camus was only a philosopher; he himself never lived the life of a rebel. He lived the life of a very respectable man, honored by the society with a Nobel Prize, honored around the world as a great thinker, novelist, a creative genius. If he had lived the life of a rebel he would have been on the cross. Can you ever conceive of Jesus Christ receiving a Nobel Prize? His prize will always be crucifixion.

One of my disciples got a Nobel Prize for economic theories; he also served on the Nobel Prize committee. Being my sannyasin, listening to me and reading my books, he spoke with the king of Sweden, who is the president of the Nobel Prize committee. He said to him, "You have given me a Nobel Prize—what about my master?"

And the king said, "Never, never again mention his name, because that will destroy your credibility with the Nobel Prize committee. They will throw you out." And when he informed me of what happened, that they are not even ready to listen to my name, I said, "That's perfectly right, I don't belong to these people who get Nobel Prizes; I belong to those people who get crucifixions. If there is any committee that crucifies people, then my name will be on the top of the list."

It is not only the case with Camus but with all philosophers. They come very close to great insights, but they never practice them; hence they remain beautiful ideas in their books—people enjoy them.

> Father and son, both great philosophers and both as lazy as possible, were sprawled in their chairs one day. The father said, "Simon, go out and see if it is raining."
>
> "Pa," said Simon, "can't you call in the dog and see if he is wet?"

No philosopher is ready to go out, even to see whether it is raining or not. As a philosopher, Camus had many insights which may look similar to mine—they are, but he is only a philosopher. I am a rebel, not a philosopher, and that makes such a difference—exactly the difference between a Nobel Prize and crucifixion.

Ten

Meditation Brings Utopia to Earth

Osho,

The longing for a better life, for a utopia, has been constantly in man's mind since he became aware of his consciousness. On the other hand, he became more and more afraid of all his irrational powers. Can you please comment?

The yearning for a utopia is basically the yearning for harmony in the individual and in the society. The harmony has never existed; there has always been a chaos. Society has been divided into different cultures, different religions, different nations...and all based on superstitions. None of the divisions are valid. But these divisions show that man is divided within himself; these are the projections of his own inner conflict. He is not one within, that's why he could not create one society, one humanity outside.

The cause is not outside. The outside is only the reflection of the inner man.

Man has developed from the animals. Even if Charles Darwin is not right... his theory of evolution, that man has developed out of the apes, does look a little childish, because for thousands of years these apes have been there, but none of them have developed into human beings. So it is strange that only a few apes developed into human beings and the remaining ones still are apes; and there seems to be no sign that they are going to change into human beings.

Secondly, he could not find a link between man and the ape, because whenever things develop there are always steps, not jumps. The ape cannot simply jump and become a human being. There must be a process of evolution; there must be a few in-between stages, and those stages are missing. Charles Darwin worked his whole life to find the missing link, but he could not find anything.

But according to Eastern mysticism, in a very different way man is evolved from the animals—not as far as his body is concerned, but as far as his being is concerned. And that seems to be more relevant. Charles Darwin has almost lost his ground in scientific fields. Now the anti-Darwinians are winning, and Charles Darwin is almost out of date. It was only a fiction. But Eastern mysticism has the same theory—not that the ape's body develops into a human body, but that an ape's soul, or an elephant's soul, or a lion's soul, can develop into a human being. First the soul develops and then, according to the soul's need, nature provides the body. So there is no bodily evolution but there is a spiritual connection.

This is profoundly supported by modern psychoanalysis, particularly Carl Gustav Jung's school, because in the collective unconscious of man there are memories which belong to animalhood. If man is taken deep into hypnosis, first he enters the unconscious mind, which is just the repressed part of this life. If he is hypnotized even more deeply, then he enters into the collective unconscious, which has memories of being animals. People start screaming—in that stage they cannot speak a language. They start moaning or crying, but language is impossible; they can shout, but in an animal way. And in the collective unconscious state, if they are allowed to move or they are told to move, they move on all fours, they don't stand up. In the collective unconscious there are certainly remnants that suggest that they have been at some time in some animal body. And different people come from different animal bodies. That may be the cause of such a difference in individuals. And sometimes you can see a similarity—somebody behaves like a dog, somebody behaves like a fox, somebody behaves like a lion.

And there is great support in folklore, in ancient parables like Aesop's Fables, or Panchtantra in India, which is the most ancient, in which all the stories are about animals, but are very significant for human beings and represent certain human types.

Charles Darwin may have failed because he was only looking for a link between bodies, physical bodies. There may not be any link between physical bodies, but Eastern mysticism may be right that man has evolved spiritually from animalhood.

Man still carries much of the animal's instinct—his anger, his hatred, his jealousy, his possessiveness, his cunningness. All that has been condemned in man seems to belong to a very deep-rooted unconscious. And the whole work of spiritual alchemy is how to get rid of the animal past.

Without getting rid of the animal past, man will remain divided. The animal past and his humanity cannot exist as one, because humanity has just the opposite qualities. So all that man can do is become a hypocrite. As far as formal behavior is concerned, he follows the ideals of humanity—of love and of truth, of freedom, of nonpossessiveness, compassion. But it remains only a very thin layer, and at any moment the hidden animal can come up; any accident can bring it up. And whether it comes up or not, the inner consciousness is divided.

This divided consciousness has been creating the yearning and the question: How to become a harmonious whole as far as the individual is concerned? And the same is true about the whole society: How can we make the society a harmonious whole, where there is no war, no conflict, no classes, no divisions of color, caste, religion, nation?

Because of people like Thomas Moore, who wrote the book *Utopia*, the name became synonymous with all idealistic goals—but they have not grasped the real problem. That's why it seems their idea of a utopia is never going to happen. If you think of society as becoming an ideal society, a paradise, it seems to be impossible. There are so many conflicts, and there seems to be no way to harmonize them. Every religion wants to conquer the whole world, not to be harmonized. Every nation wants to conquer the whole world, not to be harmonized. Every culture wants to spread all over the world and to destroy all other cultures, not to bring a harmony between them.

So utopia became synonymous with something which is simply imaginary. And there are dreamers—the very word *utopia* also means "that which is never going to happen." But still man goes on thinking in those terms again and again. There seems to be some deep-rooted urge...but man's thinking is about the symptoms; that's why it seems that utopia is never going to happen. He is not looking at the causes. The causes are within individuals.

Utopia is possible. A harmonious human society is possible, should be possible, because it will be the best opportunity for everyone to grow, the best opportunity for everyone to be himself. The richest possibilities will be available to everyone. So it seems that the way it is, society is absolutely stupid. The utopians are not dreamers, but your so-called realists who condemn utopians are stupid. But both are agreed on one point—that something has to be done in the society.

Prince Kropotkin, Bakunin, and their followers, would like all the governments to be dissolved—as if it is in their hands, as if you simply say so and the governments will dissolve. These are the anarchists, who are the best utopians. Reading them, it seems that whatever they are saying is significant. But they have no means to materialize it, and they have no idea how it is going to happen.

And there is Karl Marx, Engels, and Lenin—the Marxists, the communists, and different schools of socialism, connected with different dreamers. Even George Bernard Shaw had his own idea of socialism, and he had a small group called the Fabian Society. He was propagating a kind of socialist world, totally different from the communist world that exists today.

There are fascists who think that it is a question of more control and more government power; just the opposite pole of anarchists, who want no government and think all the source of corruption is government. But there are people, the fascists, who want all power in the hands of dictators. They think it is because of the democratic idea that the society is falling apart, because in democracy the lowest denominator becomes the ruler. He decides who is going to rule, and he is the most ignorant one; he has no understanding. The mob decides how the society should be. So according to the fascist, democracy is only mobocracy, it is not democracy—there is no democracy possible.

According to the communists, the whole problem is simply the class division between the poor and the rich. They think that if all government power goes into the hands of the poor, and they have a dictatorship of the proletariat—when all classes have disappeared, and the society has become equal—then soon there will be no need of any state.

They are all concerned with the society, and that is where their failure lies. As I see it, utopia is not something that is not going to happen, it is something that is possible, but we should go to the causes, not to the symptoms. And the causes are in the individuals, not in the society.

For example, seventy years passed in Soviet Russia, and the communist revolution was not able to dissolve the dictatorship. Lenin was thinking that ten or fifteen years at the most would be enough, because by that time we would have equalized everybody, distributed wealth equally; then there would be no need for a government. But after fifteen years, they found that the moment you remove the enforced state, people are going to become again unequal. There will be again rich people and there will be again poor people, because there is something in people that makes them rich or poor. So you have to keep them in almost a concentration camp if you want them to remain equal. But this is a strange kind of equality, because it destroys all freedom, all individuality.

And the basic idea was that the individual will be given equal opportunity. His needs should be fulfilled equally. He will have everything equal to everybody else. He will share it. But the ultimate outcome is just the opposite. They almost destroyed the individual to whom they were trying to give equality and freedom, and everything good that should be given to individuals. The very individual is removed; they have become afraid of the individual. The reason is that they are still not aware that however long the enforced state lasts, seventy or seven hundred years, it will not make any difference. The moment you remove control, there will be a few people who know how to be rich, and there will be a few people who know how to be poor. And they will simply start the whole thing again.

In the beginning they tried... because Karl Marx's idea was that there should be no marriage in communism. And he was very factual about it: that marriage was born because of individual property. His logic was correct. There was a time when there was no marriage. People lived in tribes, and just as animals make love, people made love.

The problem started only when a few people who were more cunning, more clever, more powerful, had managed some property. Now they wanted their property, after their death, to go to their own children. It is a natural desire that if a person works his whole life and gathers property, land, or creates a kingdom, it should go to his children. In a subtle way, through the children, because they are his blood, he will be still ruling, he will be still possessing. It is a way to find some substitute for immortality, because the continuity will be there: "I will not be there, but my child will be there, who will represent me, who will be my blood and my bones and my marrow. This child will be a continuity, so in a subtle sense, I will have immortality. I cannot live forever, so this is a substitute way."

That's why marriage was created; otherwise it was easier for man not to have any marriage, because marriage was simply a responsibility—of children, of a wife. When the woman is pregnant, then you have to feed her, and there was no need to take all that responsibility. The woman was taking the whole responsibility for herself. But the man wanted some immortality, and that his property should be possessed by his own blood. The woman wanted some protection, she was vulnerable. While she was pregnant she could not work, she could not go hunting; she had to depend on somebody. So it was in the interest of both to have a contract that they would remain together, would not betray in any sense, because the whole thing was to keep the blood pure.

So Marx's idea was that when communism comes, and property becomes collective, marriage becomes meaningless because its basic reason is removed—now you don't have any private property. Your son will not have anything as an inheritance. In fact, just as you cannot have private property, you cannot have a private woman; that too is property. And you cannot have a private son or daughter, because that too is private property. So with the disappearance of private property, marriage will disappear.

So after the revolution, for two or three years, in Russia they tried it, but it was impossible. Private property had disappeared, but people were not ready to drop marriage. And even the government found that if marriage disappears, the whole responsibility falls on the government for the children, the woman. So why take on unnecessary responsibility?—and it is not a small thing. It is better to let marriage continue. So they reversed the policy; they forgot all about Karl Marx, because just within three years they found that this was going to create difficulty, and people were not willing.

People were not willing to drop private property, either—it was forcibly taken away from them. Almost one million people were killed for small private properties. Somebody had a small piece of land, a few acres, and everything was going to be nationalized. Although the people were poor, still they wanted to cling to their property. At least they had something, and now even that was going to be taken out of their hands. They were hoping to get something more—that's why they had supported the revolution and fought for it. Now what they had was going to be taken out of their hands. It was going to become government property, it was going to be nationalized. And for small things—somebody may have had just a few hens, or a cow, and he was not willing to give them up, because that was all that he had. A small house... he was not willing for it to be nationalized.

These poor people—one million people were killed to make the whole country aware that nationalization had to happen. Even if you had only a cow and you didn't give it to the government, you were finished. And the government was thinking that people would be willing to separate... but this is how the merely theoretical and logical people have always failed to understand man. They have never looked into his psychology.

This was true, that marriage was created after private property came into being; marriage followed it. Logically, as private property is dissolved, marriage should disappear. But they don't understand the human mind. As property was taken away, people became even more possessive of each other because nothing else was left. Their land has gone, their animals have gone, their houses have gone. Now they don't want to lose their wife or their husband or their children. This is too much.

Logic is one thing... and unless we try to understand man more psychologically and less logically, we are always going to commit mistakes. Marx was proved wrong. When everything was taken away, people were clinging to each other more, more than before, because now that was their only possession: a woman, a husband, children. And it was such a gap in their life; their whole property had gone and now their wife was also to be nationalized? They could not conceive the idea because their mind and their tradition said, "That is prostitution." Their children had to be nationalized—they had not fought the revolution for this.

So, finally the government had to reverse the policy. In the first constitution they had declared that now there shall be no marriage, and the question of divorce did not arise. Just within three years they had to change it. And after that, marriage became more strict than anywhere else. Divorce became more difficult than anywhere else, because the government did not want unnecessary changes. Divorce creates paperwork and more bureaucracy, so the government wanted people to remain together, not to unnecessarily change partners. And divorce creates legal cases about the children, who should have them, the father or mother; it is unnecessary. The government thinks of efficiency—less bureaucracy, less paperwork—and people are creating unnecessary paperwork, so it became very difficult to get a divorce.

And as time passed, they found that there was no way to keep people equal without force. But what kind of a utopia is it that is kept by force? And because the communist party had all the force, a new kind of division came into being, a new class of bureaucrats: those who had power, and those who didn't have any power. And it was very difficult to become a member, to obtain membership of the communist party in the Soviet Union, because that would be entering into the power elite. The communist party created many other groups—first you have to be a member of those groups, and you have to be checked in every way. When they find that you are really reliable, absolutely reliable, trustworthy, then you may enter into the communist party.

The party wants to remain as small as possible so that the power is in a few hands.

The people were never so powerless under a capitalist regime or under a feudal regime. Under the czars they were never so powerless. It was possible for a poor man, if he was intelligent enough, to become rich. Now it was not so easy. You may be intelligent, but it is not so easy to enter from the powerless class into a class which holds power. The distance between the two classes was far more than it was before.

There is always a mobility in a capitalist society, because there are not only poor people and rich people; there is a big middle class, and the middle class is continuously moving. A few people of the middle class are moving into the super-rich, and more people are moving into the poor class. A few poor people are moving into the middle class; a few rich people are falling into the middle class, or may even fall into the poor class... there is mobility. In a communist society there is an absolutely static state. Classes are now completely cut off from each other. They were going to create a classless society, and they created the most strict society with static classes.

It is almost a repetition of Hinduism. What Manu did five thousand years ago, communists did in the Soviet Union. Manu made Hindu society into four classes. There is no mobility. You are born a *Brahmin*; that is the only way to be a *Brahmin*. And that is the highest society, the topmost class. Then number two is the warriors, the kings, the *chhatriyas*. But you are born in that caste, it is not a question that you can move. Then the third is the class of the *vaishyas*, the businesspeople; you are born in it. And the fourth is the *sudras*, the untouchables. All are born into their caste. That's why, until Christianity started converting so many Hindus, particularly the *sudras*, who were ready, very willing to become Christians, because at least they would be touchable.... Amongst Hindus sudras are untouchable, and there is no way to get out of the structure.

For your whole life you have to remain the same as your forefathers remained for five thousand years. For five thousand years there has been a stratified society. If somebody is a shoemaker, his family has been making shoes for five thousand years. He cannot do any other work, he cannot enter into any other profession. That is not allowed.

Hindus were not a converting religion, because the great question was, if you convert somebody, in what class are you going to put the person? Christianity is a converting religion because it has no classification; you simply become a Christian. If Catholics convert you, you become a Catholic; if Protestants convert you, you become a Protestant. But in Hinduism you cannot be converted, because where will you be put? Brahmins won't allow you, and you would not like to be put with the sudras, the untouchables. So then what is the point of coming to a religion where you will not be even touched? Even your shadow will be untouchable. A Brahmin has to take a bath if the shadow of a sudra falls on him. The sudra has not touched him, but his shadow is also untouchable.

Being the most ancient religion, still Hinduism has not been spreading; it has been shrinking. Buddhism spread all over Asia, and it is only twenty-five centuries old. Hinduism is at least ten thousand years old, or more, but it could not spread, for the simple reason that birth is decisive. You can be a Hindu only by birth, just as you can be a Jew only by birth—and these are the two most ancient religions. These are really the two basic religions.

Christianity and Mohammedanism are offshoots of Judaism, and Jainism and Buddhism are offshoots of Hinduism. Jainism and Buddhism are both the rebellion of the second class—the chhatriyas, the warriors—because they had the powers. They were the kings, they were the soldiers, they had the power—and yet the Brahmin was on top of them. So naturally, sooner or later they were going to revolt, and finally they did revolt. Gautam Buddha and Mahavira are both from the second class. They wanted to be first class, they had the power, and the Brahmins had nothing; why should they be the highest class? So it was a rebellion.

But it was a strange thing that although these two religions got out of the Hindu fold, only Buddhism could spread all over Asia. Jainism could not spread out of India. Buddhism managed to spread out of India; from India it disappeared, but it took over the whole of Asia. And the reason was that it was through Gautam Buddha's very compassionate mind that he allowed anybody to enter into Buddhism.

Jainas, although they had also rebelled against the Brahmins, remained of the same mind—that they are higher than the other two classes. They wanted to be higher than Brahmins, too, but they never started converting anybody, because who would they convert? Brahmins will not be ready to be converted, they are already higher than everybody. Only sudras can be converted because they will be raised on the evaluation scale. But Jainas—Mahavira and his group—were not so compassionate as to take them in. So Jainism is not a complete culture; it has to depend on Hinduism for everything—it has remained only a philosophy. No Jaina can make shoes; some Hindu sudra has to make the shoes. No Jaina can clean the toilets; some sudra has to do that work. Although they rebelled against

Brahmins, their rebellion was just against the superiority of the Brahmins, and they wanted themselves to be higher than the Brahmins. But they were also not in favor of the lower classes being taken higher.

And the ultimate result was that Jainas have remained a very small religion, confined in numbers. And because they left Hinduism, rather than rising higher than Brahmins they even fell from the second category. Because they left Hinduism, they were no longer chhatriyas. They were no longer considered to be warriors, and they could not be, because of their nonviolence. They had to drop the idea of fighting, so the only way was to become businesspeople. Lower you can go, nobody prevents you. So they went from the second class to the third class and they all became businesspeople. So the rebellion failed very badly. Jainas wanted to become higher than the first class; the outcome of their revolution was that they went from the second class to the third class.

And they are absolutely dependent on Hindus. For their manual work they need workers—they cannot work. And because they became businesspeople, slowly, slowly the Hindu businesspeople and the Jaina businesspeople came closer. Even marriages started happening between them. By and by, they even had to ask Brahmins to do their worship work—and they had money to pay for it. So Brahmins worshipped for the Jainas—who are against Brahmanism, against Hinduism, but they had to use Hindus for everything. Their shoes are made by the sudras, their toilets are cleaned by the sudras. Their properties have to be protected by the chhatriyas, because they cannot take a sword in their hands. They cannot kill, so they cannot fight, they cannot go to war; they have their security force in the warrior caste. And finally their priests—the Brahmins came in from the back door as their priests.

Manu tried this immobile society, which is still the same, five thousand years ago. That too was a kind of utopia, because he was thinking in terms of there being no class struggle this way.

The class struggle can be dropped in two ways. Either there should be no classes; then there will be no class struggle.... That's what communism is doing, but it has failed because a new class has appeared. The other way is that the classes should be so stratified that there is no question of one person moving into another class. No struggle will be there, so there will be no competition. The Brahmin will remain a Brahmin. He will remain on the top; whether he is poor or rich does not matter. The businessman will remain a businessman. Just because he is rich he cannot become a Brahmin, he cannot purchase the caste. He cannot rise; he will remain third class, however rich he is. The sudras will remain sudras: they have to do all the dirty work and they cannot move from there.

This was also a utopia. The idea was that if the classes are completely static, there is not going to be any struggle, competition. In a way, Manu succeeded more than Marx, because for five thousand years his idea has remained in practice, and in India the Hindu society has never been in a class struggle. The poor are there, the rich are there, but that is not the real problem for the Hindu. His real problem is those four classes, which are absolutely static. But that is very dangerous because you prevent people from moving in a direction where they can find their potential fulfilled. A sudra may prove to be a great warrior, but he will never be allowed. A Brahmin may prove a great industrialist, but he cannot lower himself. So it saved the society from class struggle, but it destroyed the individual and his potential completely. The genius was ruined. In just the same way it is happening in communism: the individual is destroyed, his genius is ruined. He cannot move upwards even if he has the capacity.

There have been attempts all over the world to make a harmonious human society, but all have failed for the simple reason that nobody has bothered why it is not naturally harmonious. It is not harmonious because each individual inside is divided, and his divisions are projected onto the society. And unless we dissolve the individual's inner divisions, there is no possibility of really realizing a utopia and creating a harmonious society in the world.

The only way for a utopia to happen is that your consciousness should grow more, and your unconsciousness should grow less, so finally a moment comes in your life when there is nothing left that is unconscious. You are simply a pure consciousness; then there is no division. And this kind of person, who has just consciousness and nothing opposed to it, can become the very brick in creating a society which has no divisions. In other words, only a society which is enlightened enough can fulfill the demand of being harmonious—a society of enlightened people, a society of great meditators who have dropped their divisions.

Instead of thinking in terms of revolution and changing the society, its structure, we should think more of meditation and changing the individual. That is the only possible way that some day we can drop all divisions in the society—first they have to be dropped in the individual. And they *can* be dropped there.

It is almost like the fourfold division as Manu conceived the society. You have the conscious, you have the unconscious, you have the collective unconscious, and you have the cosmic unconscious. These are the four divisions within you; as you go deeper you go into darker spaces. Manu also divided society in four. The most conscious part is the Brahmin—he is the uppermost, the wisest part. But Manu starts with the society. When he first divided the society, somebody may have been a wise man, but it is not necessary that his sons and daughters will also be wise, that generation after generation the wise man will create only wise people—that is a stupid idea. So the first division may have been accurate. He may have sorted out people correctly: the conscious people on the top, then less conscious people, then more unconscious people, then absolutely unconscious people. And if Manu calls absolutely unconscious people "sudras," untouchables, there is nothing wrong in it; philosophically, it is absolutely right. But practically speaking, he went wrong because he did not consider that it would not always happen that the unconscious people would produce unconscious people.

It happened that all the enlightened people came from the second class—that is, from the warriors, not from the Brahmins, which were the topmost class. It is strange. Even Hindu incarnations like Rama and Krishna belonged to the second class; they were not Brahmins. Buddha and Mahavira—they were not Brahmins. So the Brahmin class has not produced a single enlightened person, because they became self-satisfied. They were on the top—what more do you need? Everybody was going to touch their feet; even the king had to touch their feet. They were the purest people, so there was no urge on their part to find more; it was enough. It was very satisfying and gratifying to their egos.

Why did it happen to the *chhatriyas*, the second class? My understanding is that because they were second class, there was an immense urge for them to surpass the Brahmins, and the only way they could find to surpass the Brahmins was to become enlightened. Then only could they surpass the Brahmins; otherwise they could not.

The Brahmins are the most learned scholars. The *chhatriyas* had to attain something higher than learning and scholarship. They had to attain something which is not given by birth, so Brahmins cannot claim it. Just by birth nobody can claim enlightenment. So it only happened in the second class because it is part of human psychology that the closer you are to the highest class, the more competitiveness is within you. The more distant you are the less hope you have that you can manage to compete with the Brahmin. The businessman cannot think he can manage to compete. The sudra, of course, cannot even imagine or dream that he can manage anything. He is not allowed even to read; he is not allowed to be educated. He is kept completely enslaved in his unconsciousness, so there is no question of a sudra becoming enlightened.

The businessman has another competition, and that is of money. That is a horizontal competition among businessmen. He is trying to compete to have more money, and he knows he cannot compete with the warriors: a businessman is not a soldier. He cannot compete with the priest, because a businessman is not a scholar, and the Brahmins kept a complete hold on all the great ancient scriptures and literature. They were only to give those books to their children, to their descendants. For thousands of years those books were not printed, even though printing started in China three thousand years ago and it could have come to India without any difficulty. People must have been aware of printing, they were constantly coming and going to China. If Buddhism could spread all over China, it is impossible that those travelers could not have brought back the mechanism and the understanding needed to print. But Brahmins were against printing. They were even against printing their scriptures when the Britishers came three hundred years ago and took over India from the Mohammedans. It was against the Brahmins' will that the scriptures be printed, because they were afraid that once they were printed, they would become public property. Then anybody could read them, and anybody could become a scholar. They wanted to keep them to themselves, so there were only handwritten copies of the scriptures, kept as a family heritage: each family had its own handwritten copy of certain scriptures. The Brahmins monopolized it.

The *chhatriyas*, the second class, tried—and it was a great effort—to become enlightened, to surpass the Brahmins. But it is very significant to understand that by becoming enlightened they became divisionless, their being became one. And certainly they became higher than any human being who was divided. There was no question about their superiority. So even Brahmins would come to the enlightened people without bothering that they came from the second class. Brahmins have touched the feet of non-Brahmins—which would have been impossible in Manu's system. But once the non-Brahmin has become enlightened, then the Brahmin knows that what he knows is only parrot-like. What this enlightened man knows is not parrot-like. He is not a scholar, he is really a knower. So hundreds of Brahmins were disciples of Buddha, hundreds of Brahmins were disciples of Mahavira.

The world can come to a harmony if meditation is spread far and wide, and people are brought to one consciousness within themselves. This will be a totally different dimension to work with.

Up to now it was revolution. The point was society, its structure. It has failed again and again in different ways. Now it should be the individual—and not revolution, but meditation, transformation. And it is not so difficult as people think. They may waste six years in getting a master's degree in a university; and they will not think that this is wasting too much time for just a degree which means nothing. It is only a question of understanding the value of meditation. Then it is easily possible for millions of people to become undivided within themselves. They will be the first group of humanity to become harmonious. And their harmoniousness, their beauty, their compassion, their love, all their qualities are bound to resound around the world.

My effort is to make meditation almost a science, so it is not something to do with religion. So anybody can practice it—whether he is a Hindu or a Christian or a Jew or a Mohammedan doesn't matter. What his religion is, is irrelevant; he can still meditate. He may not even believe in any religion, he may be an atheist; still he can meditate.

Meditation has to become almost like a wildfire. Then there is some hope.

And people are ready: they have been thirsting for something that changes the whole flavor of the society. It is ugly as it is, it is disgusting. It is at the most, tolerable. Somehow people have been tolerating it. But to tolerate is not a very joyful thing. It should be ecstatic, it should be enjoyable. It should bring a dance to people's hearts.

And once these divisions within a person disappear, he can see so clearly about everything. It is not a question of his being knowledgeable, it is a question of his clarity. He can look at every dimension, every direction, with such clearness, with such deep sensitivity, perceptiveness, that he may not be knowledgeable but his clarity will give you answers knowledge cannot give.

The idea of utopia is one of the most important things that has been following man like a shadow for thousands of years. But somehow it got mixed up with the changing of society; the individual never got looked at. Nobody has paid much attention to the individual, and that is the root cause of all the problems. But because the individual seems to be so small, and the society seems so big, people think that we can change society and then the individuals will change.

This is not going to be so—because "society" is only a word; there are only individuals, there is no society. The society has no soul; you cannot change anything in it. You can change only the individual, howsoever small he appears. And once you know the science of how to change the individual, it is applicable to all the individuals everywhere. And my feeling is that one day we are going to attain a society which will be harmonious, which will be far better than all the ideas that utopians have been producing for thousands of years.

The reality will be far more beautiful.

Eleven

Rest in Peace – or in Pieces

Osho,

I have heard you say that people are attracted to war because it is exciting, whereas peace is boring. In my own experience, I seem to enjoy indulging my personal dramas and traumas, and when I'm not indulging them life is a bit flat. Is it possible to be attracted to peace? Will the new humanity find peace, rather than war, exciting?

It has never happened. Man has never found peace exciting. It seems that the way man is, war certainly will remain exciting, because the peace that you know is not the real peace; it is the peace of a cemetery, not the peace of this place where we are meeting now! No war is going on, everything is silent —do you think it is flat? The new man will know this peace twenty-four hours round the clock, waking or sleeping. And the peace that is not only absence of war but a positive flowering within you, a positive, wordless song within you, is totally different.

Up to now man has known peace, but that peace was only preparation for war. History can be divided into two parts: the period when people are fighting, and the period when people are exhausted, tired, ruined, preparing for another war from scratch. War or preparation for war: these are the only two periods human history has known up to now. Peace has never been known because peace is something which the individual has to create. War is something which the crowd, the nation, the politician, the ideologies, the churches create. Peace, each individual has to create. It will be far better to say that he has to discover it, because it has not to be created; it is already there inside you but you are surrounded so much by the mind and its turmoil, you never come to hear the still, small voice within you.

And if you cannot hear even the still, small voice within you, how can you taste peace, which is beyond that voice, where you simply exist? There is no thought in the mind, no emotion in the heart. In that nothingness you come to know, for the first time, the taste of peace.

I am saying it from my own experience. For thirty-two years I have been in that peace, and I have not found it for a single moment flat. It is always opening new doors, new dimensions, new depths.

When for the first time you know your inner peace, you think, "This is the end." Soon you have to change this idea, because the peace goes on growing. And the day comes when you understand that there is no end; the peace is going to become as vast as the universe itself—and the universe has no limits.

You must be feeling flat when you are not passing through some drama or trauma, because in your life what else have you got? If there is nothing going on—a fight, a love affair, a marriage, a divorce, fighting for an election or going bankrupt—if all these things are not going on around you, naturally you feel flat. It seems nothing is happening, time has stopped; you feel dead.

It is a well-established fact that whenever there is war in the world, wherever it is, people look more happy, excited. They wake up early in the morning, waiting for the newspaper to come. What is happening? What has happened last night? They cannot wait, they want to know it immediately. People carry their radios glued to their ears not to miss a single bit of information. Life is no longer flat, there is excitement, because every moment something new is happening—victory or defeat, something is happening; you can look forward to some news. When there is no war, then tomorrow's newspaper will be carrying exactly the same as today's news.

I used to live in a place... just opposite my house lived the family of a doctor. The doctor was thought to be a little crazy; still, he was a good doctor. People used to come to him, knowing perfectly well that he was a little crazy but as far as his profession was concerned, he was perfectly sane. He used to come every day in the early morning to my house, to read all the newspapers and magazines available there. He would come and ask for the latest newspaper.

One day I gave him a newspaper of the same date, but from the year before. And he enjoyed it, he loved it! He said he had never expected these things to happen, because they didn't seem to be connected with yesterday's newspaper.

I said, "Now that I know that, every day you will be excited."

He said, "But how did you do it?"

I said, "This newspaper is one year old."

He said, "My God! If reading old newspapers makes you so excited, why have you been keeping it a secret from me? Sometimes I used to wonder why you go on collecting old newspapers, magazines. Now I know! Now I don't care whether today's newspaper comes or not. There are so many piled up in your room. I can pull one out from anywhere, and it will be exciting."

People are excited with something that is unexpected. Politicians rule over you because they provide excitement. Wars have been condemned for centuries but nobody listens, because everybody knows that a long peace will be so flat—people will start committing suicide, there is nothing happening.

Just think of one year... no news happens. You just go on waiting and waiting and waiting. Then finally you decide to create news yourself: you commit suicide or you murder somebody. Something has to be done to break this peace.

In one of the dramas of an existentialist philosopher, a man is brought before the court because he has killed a stranger, someone whom he had never known before. He had not even seen the man's face. The man was sitting on the beach looking at the sea, and this fellow came from behind with a big dagger and pushed it into his back. He had never seen that man before; he did not even see him while he was murdering him. What could be the cause?—because that stranger was absolutely innocent.

The man was, of course, caught and presented before a court. The judge was also puzzled. He inquired of a few witnesses, "Is this man mad?"

They said, "No. In our neighborhood, this is the most rational and sane man." The judge was trying to find out something in his past which could make some sense of this act which he had done.

One man said, "I remember one thing, that when his mother died, it was Sunday morning, and we were both sitting in the garden. He said, 'I knew that old bitch was going to spoil my beautiful holy day. Now, couldn't she have died on Friday, or Tuesday, or Monday? Why on Sunday? I was ready to go boating on the lake, and I have to cancel my whole program.'"

The neighbor said, "That day I thought this man was strange. His mother dies and he says, 'That woman died purposely on Sunday. She was always making efforts to spoil all my happiness. Even in death she continued her old habit.'"

Another witness said, "When all the proceedings for the funeral were over, this man immediately rushed to the house of his girlfriend, and they went to see a movie. In the morning, the mother dies; by the evening, he is at a movie with his girlfriend."

A third witness said, "That is nothing, because after the movie, he was drinking and dancing! His behavior has always been a little bizarre."

The magistrate asked the man himself, "Do you have any explanation for these things?"

He said, "For everything that I have done I have explanations. My mother dies on Sunday morning: my Sunday, my plan to go to the lake is spoiled—is it wrong to say it clearly, rather than repress it? And anyway whether I say it or not, my mother is dead, so what difference does it make?

"And certainly I was angry. She could have died... there are seven days in the week—why choose Sunday especially? And she knew, because the previous night I had told her, 'Tomorrow morning I am going to the lake.' And I am absolutely certain she died on purpose because she was the only one who knew that I was going to the lake in the morning. And as I was preparing to leave, she died. You think I have to give an explanation, or does that dead woman have to give an explanation?"

The magistrate said, "Okay. About that nothing can be done; your mother is dead, she cannot be asked. It may have been just a coincidence. But does it look right to you that in the morning your mother dies and in the evening you go to a movie? And in the night you are found in a nightclub drinking, dancing—do you think it looks right?"

He said, "Absolutely right. Because now, whenever I go to a movie it will be after my mother's death. Do you mean that for the rest of life I cannot go to a movie? Whenever I go to the nightclub and drink and dance, it will be after my mother's death. Do you want me to commit suicide because now I cannot enjoy anything, since it is after my mother's death? What difference does it make whether her death was ten hours ago or ten days ago, or ten years ago?"

There was great silence in the court. The man looked rational, what he was saying was meaningful. "Now everything I am going to do is going to be after my mother's death! What do you want me to do? Should I also die with my mother because now there is no point in living any longer; will I be a criminal if I live? If I laugh, somebody will say, 'What? You are laughing, and your mother is dead?' And the time factor... can you tell me what is the demarcation line? Ten hours, twelve hours, ten days, twelve days, ten years, twelve years? What is the criterion to decide that now it is all right to dance and drink—now I can let my mother be dead.

"I thought that if I am to love, I have to accept the fact that my mother is dead; and then there is no point in wasting time. Moreover, I had purchased those two tickets already.

Wasting those two tickets over a dead person, I don't think is sane."

The magistrate said, "Never mind all these things. You just tell me exactly why you killed that man on the beach. You had never known him, he had never done any harm to you. You were not even aware whom you were killing."

The man said, "It is very simple. My life was going very flat. I used to think, 'Once my mother is gone there will be peace.' But once she had gone everything became flat. I would come home drunk in the middle of the night and nobody was there to nag me and instruct me as to what time to come home, what to do and what not to do. Life became flat, and I wanted some excitement. And I got it. Does it matter whom I killed?"

He said, "When I pushed the dagger into the man's back, and a fountain of blood came out, for the first time in years I was excited: what was happening? Something new! I have never seen a fountain coming out of a man's back. And such red blood! No, I do not know who the man was, I have no enmity with him. I have not killed him for any reason except for my own excitement. And I got it; since then, life has been very exciting.

"I escaped, and the police chased me; finally I was caught, then I was jailed. Things started moving! Now I am standing in the court listening to all these idiots who are my neighbors. And it gives me great joy to contradict what they are saying. It is hilarious, I have never enjoyed life so much! And I am already tremendously excited waiting for the judgment, to see whether I am released, whether I am sent to a mental hospital, or I am sentenced to death, or twenty years' imprisonment. There are so many alternatives in my mind."

This man is you.

People are doing all kinds of things just to feel excited. And when the whole world becomes dull, starts feeling stale, flat, some politician comes as a savior to you, an Adolf Hitler. Many people in the world are waiting for another Adolf Hitler—life is becoming flat. That man Hitler made the five years from 1940 to 1945 tremendously exciting. I don't think there has ever been such a long period so full of excitement for the whole world. Adolf Hitler should be given as many Nobel Prizes as possible for making the whole world alive, thriving, their hearts beating faster. They are still waiting for another one.

I received a letter from the American Nazi party. Can you think that in America there is a Nazi party? I got the letter from the president of the party, and he was very angry, "Because," he said, "you have been continually speaking against Adolf Hitler; and it hurts our religious feelings." Even I was excited! This is really great: "religious feelings"?

So many years have passed since the second world war. The credit does not go to you, the credit goes to the nuclear weapons, because the parties which are capable of fighting are afraid. They know perfectly well that in nuclear war, nobody is going to win, that everybody is going to be finished forever. The whole of life on the earth is going to disappear. It does not matter who starts the war—the other party will start only minutes later, so anybody can start, it does not matter. The other party will be at the most ten minutes late, and in ten minutes you cannot be victorious. You can destroy a few cities, but you cannot be victorious. Your missiles are aiming at Moscow; their missiles are aiming at New York, Washington, San Francisco—just a pushbutton game. They are frozen out of fear, that's why so many years have passed. And I know that unless the war begins accidentally, the third world war is almost impossible. It is very close, any moment it can happen, but it will be just an accident: some technological defect, some scientist getting nagged too much by his wife, some politician losing his power, his grip, some country wanting to have the attention of the whole world, some crackpot somewhere. There are so many crackpots, and most of them are in politics.

Pots without cracks don't go into politics; they have other, useful things to do. A crackpot is of no use. That's why politics is the only profession in the world where no qualification is needed; everybody is perfectly qualified.

Now there is so much power in the hands of the politicians that they themselves are afraid. They would like to win the war, but it is impossible; the nuclear parties are equally balanced. And the war is not going to be between two countries; nuclear weapons will spread it all over the world. Perhaps within twenty-four hours all life on earth will disappear. This is frightening. That's why the war has not happened, and perhaps may not happen. But it is always very close; anything can go wrong.

I was just talking to one journalist, and I was saying to him that you should not depend on machines. And now the whole war game is not between man and man—that is out of date—the whole war game is between technological weapons. Even the planes that carry the weapons will not have any pilots with them, there is no need. The missile itself can be programmed where to go, where to drop the bomb.

I was saying to this journalist that man has become so dependent on technology that anything can go wrong any moment. And when I said this, the electricity went off! The journalist had nothing to say anymore. The proof was there! I said, "Now we can move onto another subject. This is finished."

I understand that you are in a very difficult situation. You would love to live in peace, but peace seems to be flat; nothing is happening, you are almost in your grave. To avoid being in such a dead state, you go on doing something or other—falling into a love affair, chasing a man or a woman, and then the whole drama of overpowering each other, of dominating each other, fighting.... That too does not seem to be good—every night a pillow fight. It does not seem good, but excitement is there.

Every husband on his way home is thinking of excuses why he is late, figuring out where he has been, what to say, what not to say. And the woman is figuring out... she has phoned all his friends' houses and she has collected all the information that she knows he will use for his excuses. Yes, there is drama. You tell her, "I have been with one of my friends; we met after such a long time." And the woman laughs, and she says, "Don't be stupid, your friend has been here! Now I don't think your friend is a Jesus Christ who can be in two places simultaneously. You are caught." The husband feels guilty, the woman is angry, he is trying to persuade her.... At least all these dramas and traumatic experiences keep you from falling into that space you call "flat." But at such a cost! The peace is flat and the excitement is a torture; you are caught in a dilemma.

The reason is that you don't know what real peace is. Just not to fight, not to get involved again with another woman, not to go to the pub and drink too much and beat others and be beaten.... You can avoid all these things. You can just close your door and sit inside your room, but you will not find peace. The question is not of the room and you, the question is of your mind.

Your mind is born out of the monkeys—your mind is a monkey. Have you seen a monkey sitting silently? That would be a miracle! The monkey is always doing something or other, jumping from one tree to another tree in search of excitement. He is bored with peace. Even if you have not done anything, just look at the monkey and he will make faces at you. What is he doing? He is just trying to create some entertainment. He will start running after you. If you run, then he will enjoy it very much. Great excitement, although there is no point. If you stop and turn back, the monkey will go up the tree; he does not mean business, it was just a game. He was feeling flat, you were feeling flat, and it was a good game. Both became excited.

Your mind is constantly seeking and searching for some involvement, some trouble, because the peace is really killing, poisonous.

Let me repeat: this is not the peace which I am talking about. The peace I am talking about comes out of meditation; that peace comes when you come out of your mind and become centered as a witness, just watching the mind without any judgment, without any evaluation, without saying, "This is good, this is bad, this is really groovy." If you do such things, then you have already jumped in and become identified with the monkey. The moment you say, "This is groovy," you cannot remain outside; you are on the track again.

You have simply to be a witness, like a mirror that gives no judgment—a beautiful woman, a Cleopatra or an ugly Mother Teresa, it makes no difference. But the most difficult thing in your life—which should really be the easiest—is to sit by the side of the flow of your mind. Your mind is just like a river. Thoughts and thoughts and a crowd of thoughts go on passing. You simply sit on the bank, unconcerned, just a witness, and you are in for a great surprise. Slowly, slowly, as you become more and more centered and simply a witness, thoughts start disappearing. They can exist only with your identification.

You give energy to your mind. When you pull yourself out, you have stopped giving nourishment to the mind. And once there is no nourishment—thoughts are very fragile things—they start dying out. Soon there is silence, there is peace. And this peace is not the peace of a cemetery. This peace is not dead, it is not flat. It is such a tremendous experience that once you have reached the first rung of the ladder, the ladder goes to infinity. You can go on and on discovering new layers of peace. This is the real excitement, unending excitement.

That's the meaning of the word *ecstasy*: unending excitement. You cannot exhaust it, you cannot come to a point where you say, "There is no more to discover and I am feeling flat." It has never happened. On my own authority I say to you, I have been going as fast as possible, deeper and deeper into silence, but there is no bottom, there is no limit.

Each moment of silence brings new fragrance. Peace brings new flowers. Nothing is said, but much is heard. Nothing is shown, but much is seen. Nobody guides you, but some magnetic force of peace itself takes you farther and farther away from the mind, from the body, from the neighbors, from the wife, from the husband. And the excitement is continuously deepening.

Unless we can create millions of people around the earth who have experienced this kind of peace, war is inevitable, because people cannot survive flat lives. It is better to go into a war and have a little excitement, even though it means death. If a man who has not known inner peace is forced to live peacefully, he will either murder or kill himself. Even that will provide some excitement. Excitement is a great nourishment, but only the right kind of excitement is nourishment. The wrong kind of excitement is poison. And up to now humanity has been dominated by the wrong kind of excitement.

You are here with me to learn a very simple thing: to enjoy peace, to enjoy silence, to enjoy something that is within you and you do not have to depend on others for. Such a peaceful man radiates peace for others too. His silence starts touching other hearts too. His silence becomes oceanic and very inviting.

I am not fighting against the third world war, for the simple reason that there is only one way to fight it, and that is to create a peaceful humanity, a humanity which refuses to fight because now there is no excitement in fighting. Now there is excitement in sitting silently, doing nothing and letting the grass grow by itself. You have found real, authentic excitement. Now who cares to fight?

I am not directly a pacifist, I am not taking protest marches to Washington or Moscow. But I am creating and generating a force which can envelop the whole earth. And that will be the barrier against nuclear weapons, wars, and all kinds of stupidities.

Just recognize your responsibility. Man was never required to be so responsible as he is required to be today, because upon him rests the whole thing—of whether the earth is going to be alive, thriving, flowering, or is going to be a dead planet.

Twelve

The Mystery of "Yes"

Osho,

All the historical rebellions have a huge "no" at their source. Your rebellion of the soul is centered in the mystery of "yes." Will you please speak to us on the alchemy of "yes"?

There are a few very fundamental things to be understood.

First, there has never been a rebellion in the past, only revolutions. And the distinction between a revolution and a rebellion is so vast that unless you understand the difference you will not be able to figure the way out of the puzzle of your question. Once you understand the difference...

Revolution is a crowd, a mob phenomenon. Revolution is a struggle for power: one class of people who are in power are thrown out by the other class of people who have been oppressed, exploited to such a point that now even death does not matter. They don't have anything. Revolution is a struggle between the haves and the have-nots.

I am reminded of the last statement in the *Communist Manifesto* by Karl Marx. It is tremendously beautiful, and with a little change I can use it for my own purposes.

First, his exact statement: he says, "Proletariat"—his word for have-nots—"Proletariat of the world unite, and don't be afraid because you have nothing to lose except your chains."

Moments come in history when a small group of people, cunning, clever, start exploiting the whole society. All the money goes on gathering on one side and all the poverty and starvation on the other. Naturally, this state cannot be continued forever. Sooner or later those who have nothing are going to overthrow those who have all.

Revolution is a class action, it is a class struggle. It is basically political; it has nothing to do with religiousness, nothing to do with spirituality. And it is also violent, because those who have power are not going to lose their vested interest easily; it is going to be a bloody, violent struggle in which thousands, sometimes millions of people will die.

Just in the Russian revolution, thirty million people were killed. The czar's whole family—he was the king of Russia before the revolution—was killed by the revolutionaries so brutally that it is inconceivable. Even a six-month-old girl was also killed. Now, she was absolutely innocent, she had done no harm to anybody; but just because she belonged to the royal family...the whole royal family had to be destroyed completely. Seventeen people were killed, and not just killed but cut into pieces.

It is bound to happen in a revolution. Centuries of anger ultimately turns into blind violence.

And the last thing to remember: revolution changes nothing. It is a wheel: one class comes into power, others become powerless. But sooner or later the powerless are going to become the majority, because the powerful don't want to share their power, they want to have it in as few hands as possible. How long can it be tolerated? Naturally, it comes automatically. Revolution is something blind and mechanical, part of evolution. And when the powerful become the smaller group, the majority throws them away and another power group starts doing the same.

That's why I say revolution has never changed anything, or in other words, all the revolutions of history have failed. They promised much, but nothing came out of it. Even after seventy years, in the Soviet Union people were still not getting enough nourishment. Yes, there were no more the old czars and counts and countesses and princesses and princes. But in a vast ocean of poverty, even if you remove those who have power and riches it is not going to make the society rich; it is just trying to make the ocean sweet by dropping teaspoonfuls of sugar in it. All that happens is a very strange phenomenon that nobody takes notice of. Only poverty has been distributed equally: in the Soviet Union everybody became equally poor. But what kind of revolution is this? The hope was that everybody would be equally rich.

But just by hoping you cannot become rich. Richness needs a totally different ideology, of which mankind is absolutely unaware. For centuries it has praised poverty and condemned richness, comfort, luxury. Even if the poor revolt and come into power, they don't have any idea what to do with this power, how to generate energy to create more richness, comfort and luxury for people, because deep down in their minds there is a guilty feeling about richness, about luxury, about comfort. So they are in a tremendous anguish, although they have come to power. This is the moment they could change the whole structure of the society, its whole productive idea. They could bring more technology; they could drop stupid kinds of wastage.

Every country is wasting so much of its income on the army. Even the poorest countries do the same idiotic thing. But the politicians, those who are in power, are not concerned at all what happens to humanity. Their concern is whether power remains in their hands or not. They can sacrifice half of the country to death, but they will go on making efforts to have atomic weapons, nuclear missiles. It is a very insane kind of society that we have created in thousands of years. Its insanity has come now to a high peak, there is no going back. It seems we are all sitting on a volcano which can explode any moment.

Revolutions in the past have happened all around the world, but no revolution has succeeded in doing what it promised. It promised equality, without understanding the psychology of human individuality. Each human individual is so unique that to force them to equality is not going to make people happy, but utterly miserable.

I also love the idea of equality, but in a totally different way. My idea of equality is equal opportunity to all to be unequal, equal opportunity to all to be unique and themselves. Certainly they will be different from each other, and a society which does not have variety and differences is a very poor society. Variety brings beauty, richness, color.

But it has not yet dawned on the millions around the world that revolution has not helped, and they still go on thinking in terms of revolution. They have not understood anything from the history of man.

It is said that history repeats itself. I say it is not history that repeats itself; it only seems to repeat itself because man is absolutely unconscious and he goes on doing the same thing again and again without learning anything, without becoming mature, alert and aware.

When all the revolutions have failed some new door should be opened. There is no point in again and again changing the powerful into the powerless and the powerless into the powerful; this is a circle that goes on moving. I don't preach revolution, I am utterly against revolution. My word for the future, and for those who are intelligent enough in the present, is rebellion.

What is the difference?

Rebellion is individual action; it has nothing to do with the crowd. Rebellion has nothing to do with politics, power, violence. Rebellion has something to do with changing your consciousness, your silence, your being. It is a spiritual metamorphosis. And each individual passing through a rebellion is not fighting with anybody else, but is fighting only with his own darkness. Swords are not needed, bombs are not needed; what is needed is more alertness, more meditativeness, more love, more prayerfulness, more gratitude. Surrounded by all these qualities you are born anew.

I teach this new man, and this rebellion can become the womb for the new man I teach. We have tried collective efforts and they have failed. Now let us try individual efforts. And if one man becomes aflame with consciousness, joy and blissfulness, he will become contagious to many more.

Rebellion is a very silent phenomenon that will go on spreading without making any noise and without even leaving any footprints behind. It will move from heart to heart in deep silences, and the day it has reached to millions of people without any bloodshed, just the understanding of those millions of people will change our old primitive animalistic ways. It will change our greed, and the day greed is gone there is no question of accumulating money. No revolution has been able to destroy greed; those who come in power become greedy.

We have passed through a revolution in India, and it is a very significant example to understand. The people who were leading the revolution against the British rule were followers of Mahatma Gandhi, who preached poverty, who preached nonpossessiveness. The moment they came into power all his disciples started living in palaces made for viceroys. All of Gandhi's disciples, who had been thinking their whole lives that they were servants of the people, became masters of the people. Soon there was more corruption in India than anywhere else. This is very strange—this is Gandhian corruption, very religious, very pious, and the people who are doing it have been trained, disciplined to be servants of the people. But power has a tremendous capacity to change people; the moment you have power you are immediately a different person. You start behaving exactly like any other powerful person who has gone before.

I was very young when India became independent, so I have been watching this independence for many years. My whole family was involved in the freedom struggle, and when freedom came there was so much celebration all over the country. But each year the celebration became less and less, and sadness started settling.

I used to tease my father, my uncles, who had all been to jail, suffered as much as possible, and because all the elders were in the jails we suffered too, because there was nobody to look after the children. There were only women and children left, and Indian women cannot be of much help.

They cannot even come out into society; they are not capable of earning money. I know how difficult it was when all the elders of the family were thrown into jail. After the freedom I used to tease them: "Is this freedom? You destroyed your family, you destroyed yourself, you suffered and you made us suffer. Is this freedom?"

And my father used to say, "Don't say such things. We know this is not the freedom that we have been fighting for. We were thinking that when the country becomes free, everybody will enjoy freedom." But nothing has changed. Only the Britishers were gone, and in their place a single party was ruling for years. Not just a single party, but a single family—it became a dynasty, and the exploitation continues and the poverty continues. It has grown at least a hundred times more since the British Empire has been gone.

Everything has deteriorated—the morality, the character, the integrity, everything has become a commodity. You can purchase anybody; all you need is money. There is not a single individual in the whole country who is not a commodity in the marketplace; all you need is money. Everybody is purchasable—judges are purchasable, police commissioners are purchasable, politicians are purchasable. Even under British rule, India has never known such corruption.

What has the country gained? The rulers have changed, but what does that signify? Unless there is a rebelliousness spreading from individual to individual, unless we can create an atmosphere of enlightenment around the world where greed will fall down of its own accord, where anger will not be possible, where violence will become impossible, where love will be just the way you live... where life should be respected, where the body should be loved, appreciated, where comfort should not be condemned.

It is natural to ask for comfort. Even the trees...in Africa, trees grow very high; the same trees in India don't grow that high. I was puzzled, what happens? I was trying to find out why the Indian trees should grow to the same height but they don't, and the reason I found was that unless there is a density of trees, trees won't grow so high. Even at a lesser height the sun is available, and that is their comfort, that is their life, that is their joy. In Africa the jungles are so thick that every tree tries in every way to grow as high as possible, because only then can it have the joy of the sun, the joy of the rain, the joy of the wind. Only then can it dance; otherwise there is nothing but death.

The whole of nature wants comfort, the whole of nature wants all the luxury that is possible. But our religions have been teaching us against luxury, against comfort, against riches.

A man of enlightenment sees with clarity that it is unnatural to demand from people, "You should be content with your poverty, you should be content with your sicknesses, you should be content with all kinds of exploitation, you should be content and you should not try to rise higher, to reach to the sun and the rain and the wind." This is an absolutely unnatural conditioning that we are all carrying. Only a rebellion in your being can bring you to this clarity.

You say that in history all the rebellions were based on "no." Those were not rebellions; change the word. All the revolutions were based on "no." They were negative, they were against something, they were destructive, they were revengeful and violent.

Certainly, my rebellion is based on "yes"—yes to existence, yes to nature, yes to yourself. Whatever the religions may be saying and whatever the ancient traditions may be saying, they are all saying no—no to yourself, no to nature, no to existence; they are all life-negative.

My rebellion is life-affirmative. I want you to dance and sing and love and live as intensely and as totally as possible. In this total affirmation of life, in this absolute yes to nature, we can bring a totally new earth and a totally new humanity into being.

The past was "no."

The future has to be "yes."

We have lived enough with the no, we have suffered enough and there has been nothing but misery. I want people to be as joyful as birds singing in the morning, as colorful as flowers, as free as the bird on the wing with no bondages, with no conditioning, with no past—just an open future, an open sky and you can fly to the stars.

Because I am saying yes to life, all the no-sayers are against me, all over the world. My yes-saying goes against all the religions and against all the ideologies that have been forced upon man. My yes is my rebellion. The day you will be able also to say yes it will be your rebellion.

We can have rebellious people functioning together, but each will be an independent individual, not belonging to a political party or to a religious organization. Just out of freedom and out of love, and out of the same beautiful yes, we will meet. Our meeting will not be a contract, our meeting will not be in any way a surrender; our meeting will make every individual more individual. Supported by everybody else, our meeting will not take away freedom, will not enslave you; our meeting will give you more freedom, more support so that you can be stronger in your freedom. Long has been the slavery, and long has been our burden. We have become weak because of the thousands of years of darkness that have been poured on us.

The people who love to say yes, who understand the meaning of rebellion, will not be alone. They will be individuals. But the people who are on the same path, fellow-travelers, friends, will be supporting each other in their meditativeness, in their joy, in their dance, in their music. They will become a spiritual orchestra, where so many people are playing instruments but creating one music. So many people can be together and yet they may be creating the same consciousness, the same light, the same joy, the same fragrance.

It is a long way—"no" seems to be a shortcut—that's why it has not been tried up to now. Whenever I have discussed it with people, they said, "Perhaps you are right, but when will it be possible that the whole earth will say yes?"

I said, "Anyway we have been on this earth for millions of years and you have been saying no—and what is your achievement? It is time. Give a chance to yes too."

My feeling is that no is a quality of death; yes is the very center of life. No had to fail because death cannot succeed, cannot be victorious over life. If we give a chance to yes, based in rebelliousness, it is bound to become a wildfire, because everybody deep down wants it to happen. I have not found a single person in my life who does not want to live a natural, relaxed, peaceful, silent life.

But that life is possible only if everybody else is also living the same kind of life.

I can understand the fear of people that individual rebellion may take a long time, but there is no problem in it. In fact, each individual who passes through this rebellious fire becomes, at least for himself, a bliss and an ecstasy. So he has not failed; he has conquered, he has reached to the very peak of his potential. He has blossomed. There is nothing more that he can think of; the whole existence is his. As far as that individual is concerned, the rebellion is complete. He will be able to sow seeds all around. And there is no hurry; eternity is available. Slowly, slowly more and more people will become more and more conscious, more alert. Enlightenment will become a common phenomenon.

It should not be that only once in a while there is a Gautam Buddha, once in a while there is a Jesus, once in a while there is a Socrates—the names can be counted on only ten fingers. This is simply unbelievable! It is as if your garden is full of rosebushes, thousands of rosebushes, and once in a while one bush blossoms and gives you roses. And the remaining thousands stay without flowers...?

Unless a rosebush comes to blossom it cannot dance—for what? It cannot share; it has nothing to share. It remains poor, empty, meaningless. Whether it lived or not makes no difference. The only difference is when it blossoms and offers its songs and its flowers and its fragrance to existence and to anybody who is willing to receive. The rosebush is fulfilled. Its life has not been just a meaningless drag; it has become a beautiful dance full of songs, a deep fulfillment that goes to the very roots.

I am not worried about time. If the concept is understood, time is available; enough time is available.

In the East we have a beautiful proverb: The man who loses the path in the morning, if he returns home by the evening he should not be called lost. What does it matter? In the morning he went astray—just little adventures here and there—and by the evening he is back home. A few people may have come a little earlier; he has come a little late, but he is not necessarily poorer than those who have come earlier. It may be just the opposite: he may be more experienced. He has known more because he has wandered more; he has known more because he has committed more mistakes. He is much more mature and experienced because he has gone wandering so far astray. And then coming back again, falling and getting up... he is not necessarily a loser.

So time is not at all a consideration to me.

My rebellion is absolutely individual and it will spread from individual to individual. Sometime this whole planet is bound to become enlightened. Idiots may try to wait and see what happens to others, but they also finally have to join the caravan.

The very idea of enlightenment is so new, although it is not something that has not been known before. There have been enlightened people, but they never brought enlightenment as a rebellion—that is what is new about it. They became enlightened, they became contented, they became fulfilled, and a great fallacy happened and I have to point it out. Although I feel not to show any mistakes of the enlightened ones—I feel sad about it—but my responsibility is not to the dead. My responsibility is to those who are alive and to those who will be coming, so I have to make it clear.

Gautam Buddha, Mahavira, Adinatha, Lao Tzu, Kabir, all these people who became enlightened attained to tremendous beauty, to great joy, to utter ecstasy—to what I have been calling *satyam, shivam, sundram*, the truth, the godliness of the truth and the beauty of that godliness. But because they had become enlightened, they started teaching people to be contented: "Remain peaceful, remain silent." This is the fallacy. They attained contentment after a long search. It was a conclusion, not a beginning; it was the very end product of their enlightenment, but they started telling people that you can be contented right now: "Be fulfilled, be silent."

That's how they became anti-rebellious, without perhaps knowing that if a poor man remains contented with his poverty it is dangerous; if a slave remains contented with his slavery, that is dangerous.

So all the enlightened people of the past attained to great heights, about that there is no doubt. But there is a fallacy that they all perpetuated, without exception. The fallacy is that they began telling people to start with that which comes in the end. The flower comes only in the end; one has to start with the roots, with the seed. And if you tell people to start with the roses, then the only way is to purchase roses of plastic. The only way to be contented without meditation is to be a hypocrite, because deep down you are angry, deep down you are furious, deep down you want to freak out, and on the surface you are showing immense peace. This peace has been like a cancer to humanity.

You can see it happening in India more clearly than anywhere else, because the country was fortunate, blessed by more enlightened people than any other country—but unfortunately, because so many enlightened people committed the same fallacy, the country remained for twenty centuries a slave. India has remained for centuries poor, hungry, starving; no science has developed, no technology has developed. Who is responsible for all this?

Because these people were loved, respected—and they deserve to be loved and respected—when they committed fallacies, naturally nobody could imagine that they could make mistakes. Their greatest mistake was to teach people things which come only in the end; if you try to bring them in the beginning you will become simply a hypocrite, a pretender. You will start wearing a mask. On the surface you will be one person; inside you will be just the opposite, and a house divided cannot stand for long.

Man is divided into false personality and authentic individuality. Every man on the earth who is not in deep meditation is schizophrenic; there is no need for any other symptoms. It is just the natural, almost natural condition, from being told for thousands of years to be hypocrites.

The alchemy of yes can make you one, single, integrated individual. It can bring you back your lost dignity. It can bring you back the capacity to stand alone in absolute blissfulness, not needing anybody, not being dependent on anything. It will take away all your spiritual diseases—greed and jealousy and violence and lust—and it will bring a tremendous showering of all that is great, incalculably great, so great that you cannot say, "I have got it," you can only say, "Existence has given it to me." It is always a gift from the beyond; your ecstasy, your blessing, your truth, your benediction, simply shower on you.

But you will have to learn to say yes in absolute totality to nature and to existence. Your hypocrisy will not do—saying yes with your personality and deep down your individuality is saying no. What is deep down is more authentic than what shows on the surface; the surface is always made up.

> A very tight-haloed English vicar was preaching his sermon in a very snobbish English church when he kept being interrupted by a black American in the congregation.
>
> "The lord says..." began the preacher.
>
> "Far out, man!" came a cry from the back.
>
> "The rich shall perish..."
>
> "Hey man, right on!" the American called.
>
> "And the mighty shall..."
>
> "Hallelujah!" came the response from the back.
>
> The vicar managed to get to the end of his sermon, but at the end went up to the American and said, "Excuse me, I'm afraid in this country we like to keep a bit of decorum. We try to keep a stiff upper lip. It is the queen's own country, this is a place of God, and I frankly found your behavior rather disconcerting."
>
> "Hey man, I'm sorry, you are right on. I just loved the quaint way you gave us all that great shit about Moses and the Ten Commandments and I thought I would throw a few thousand greenbacks in your direction for this great thing going on here."
>
> "Far out, man!" said the preacher.

It does not take much to find out what is deep inside. All decorum, all culture is so superficial; it will be a tremendous joy to see people in their authenticity, in their reality, without any decorum, without any make-up, just as they are. The world will be tremendously benefited if all this falseness disappears.

The alchemy of yes and the rebellion based on yes are capable of destroying all that is false, and can discover all that is real and has been covered for centuries, layer upon layer by every generation, so much that even you yourself have forgotten who you are.

If suddenly somebody wakes you up in the middle of the night and asks you, "Who are you?" you will take a little time to remember who you used to be in the night before when you went to bed.

It happened that George Bernard Shaw was going to deliver a lecture some distance away from London. On the way in the train came the ticket-taker. Bernard Shaw looked in every pocket, opened all his suitcases, but the ticket was not there. Finally, he was perspiring and the ticket-taker said, "Don't be worried, I know who you are; the whole country knows, the whole world knows. The ticket must be somewhere, you don't be worried. And even if it is lost, I am here to help you get out at the station, wherever you want to get out."

George Bernard Shaw said, "Hush! I am already in confusion and you are making me more confused. I am trying to remember where I am going! Without that ticket to tell me, I have no idea!"

It is almost the same situation with everybody. You don't know who you are; your name is just a label that has been put upon you, it is not your being. Where are you going?—

you don't have any ticket to show you where you are going to get off the train, and you are just hoping that somebody may push you off somewhere, or maybe somewhere the train stops and it does not go anywhere else....

But why are you traveling in the first place? In fact, for all these fundamental questions you have only one answer: "I don't know." In this state of unawareness your revolutions cannot succeed. In this state of unawareness your desire for freedom is just a dream. You cannot understand what freedom is. For whom are you asking freedom?

My idea of a rebellion based on yes means a rebellion based on meditation, for the first time in the history of man. And because each individual has to work upon himself, there is no question of any fight, there is no question of any organization, there is no question of any conspiracy, there is no question of planting bombs and hijacking airplanes.

Some idiot at the Pune airport has put on the computer, "Beware of the sannyasins of Osho; they can hijack airplanes!" It is really a very insane world. One of my sannyasins, who has to go often to Bombay and come back, says, "Every time I see that computer I start trembling inside that they may catch hold of me and ask, 'Why do you come again and again? Are you intending to hijack an Indian Airlines airplane? It is enough that you come once— but why do you come and go at least three times in the week?'"

He was saying, "What to do? By road it seems you are going to hell, and on the airplane they have that computer. Every time I am there, immediately the computer says, 'Beware of sannyasins.'"

I am not interested in hijacking airplanes; neither am I interested in destroying any governments. But it will be the final result of my individual rebellion based on meditation: governments will disappear. They have to disappear; they have been nothing but a nuisance on the earth. Nations have to disappear. There is no need of any nations; the whole earth belongs to the whole of humanity. There is no need of any passports, there is no need of any visas.

This earth is ours, and what kind of freedom is there if we cannot even move? Everywhere there are barriers, every nation is a big imprisonment. Just because you cannot see the boundaries you think you are free. Just try to pass through the boundary and immediately you will be faced with a loaded gun: "Go back inside the prison. You belong to *this* prison. You cannot enter into another prison without permission." These are your nations!

Certainly, a rebellion of my vision will take away all this garbage of nations, and discriminations between white and black, and give the whole of humanity a natural, relaxed, comfortable life. This is possible, because science has given us everything that we need, even if the population of the earth were much greater than it is today. Just a little intelligence is needed—which will be released by meditation—and we can have a beautiful earth with beautiful people, and a multidimensional freedom which is not just a word in the dead constitutions, but a living reality.

One thing finally to be remembered: the days of revolution are past. We have tried them many times, and every time the same story is repeated. Enough. Now something new is urgently needed. And except the idea that I am giving to you of a rebellion, individual and based on meditativeness, there is no other alternative proposed anywhere in the world.

I am not a philosopher; I am absolutely pragmatic and practical. I am not only talking about meditative rebellion, I am preparing people for it. Whether they know it or not doesn't matter. Whoever comes close to me is going to become a rebellious individual, and wherever he will go he will spread this contagious health. It will make people aware of their dignity, it will make people aware of their potentiality. It will make people alert to what they can become, what they are, and why they are stuck.

My sannyasins' function is not to be missionaries but to be so loving, compassionate, such fragrant individuals... It is not a question of converting people from one ideology to another ideology. It is a far deeper transformation—from the whole past to a totally new and unknown future. It is the greatest adventure that one can think of.

You are fortunate to be part of this great adventure.

Thirteen

Gnosticism – the Roots of Religious Rebellion

Osho,

Is there any relationship between Gnosticism and anarchy?

The word *anarchism* has tremendous implications. It means that the people are so inwardly disciplined that they don't need any government. They are so deeply in order within themselves that no order outside is needed.

Anarchism is basically the transformation of the individual in such a way that the government becomes superfluous. He lives in the light of his consciousness, fully aware of what he is doing, fully aware of its consequences, aware that it is not his right to interfere with any individual's life, or to trespass—even in very subtle matters like conversion. Making an effort to convert somebody to your ideology is a trespass of that individual's consciousness. Unless he invites you, it is aggression.

So individuals have to be so conscious that no aggressive activity on any level—bodily, mental, emotional—is possible for them. Then the government is absolutely useless, a burden. And certainly the idea is that, if people can live without a government, then only are they people. If they need a government that means they are still coming out of animality. They have not yet become human. They need masters, governors, they are not capable of being on their own. They are basically asking to be slaves. The existence of a government of any kind means that the people are asking for slavery; and to ask for slavery and then to ask for democracy, freedom, freedom of expression, and individuality, becomes contradictory.

So the governments go on promising all these things, but in the very existence of the government they are denied. Hence, all governments are frauds; they can only promise, they cannot perform. It is existentially impossible. If they can perform then they are not needed. If they cannot perform—that is why they are needed. So every government is more or less symbolic of the fact that human beings have not grown up to their full height, to their full potential.

You are asking, "Are Gnosticism and anarchy in some way related?" They are... because Gnosticism means knowledge of your own. There are two kinds of knowledge. One is borrowed, either from books or from teachers, or from parents or from the environment, the society in which you live. Unconsciously you go on absorbing so many things. This is not knowledge in the sense of Gnosticism. This is a false substitute for true knowledge, and it is a hindrance. True knowledge is the discovery of truth, of love, of compassion, of all that is great in human life—by yourself.

Every Buddhist scripture begins: "I have heard Gautam the Buddha say...." It is a hearsay, it is not knowledge. You may have heard Gautam the Buddha say something—that does not mean that you have come to know it. It may become part of your memory, you may be able to repeat it like a parrot...that's all that your priests, your pundits, are doing all over the world, simply repeating exactly the way the parrot repeats without knowing what he is saying.

The pundits don't know what they are saying. They have heard, they have memorized; their memory is good, but their intelligence does not exist.

True knowledge means your own experience, your own search—and when you know yourself, there is no need to believe in anything. Every belief is poisonous because every belief will hinder you in searching for the truth.

Now the whole world believes in something or other. You ask anybody about God—either he believes that God exists... and there are a few who believe that God does not exist, but both are beliefs. The communist believes that God does not exist, but he has not explored. He has not gone into his own consciousness, what to say about the whole of existence? He has not explored even his own small being.

And there are millions who say, "We believe in the existence of God." But your belief cannot create a God—if he does not exist, your belief makes no difference. And if you believe in a God, naturally your seeking stops. Why should one seek and search when he believes? That's why all the religions emphasize faith, so that they can stop your search.

Faith is a block. Search means you are still doubting, you are still not certain. Faith means you are absolutely certain that God exists; now there is no question of enquiring. And if a man goes on believing in such things, which imply many absurdities.... For example, Galileo was told by the pope, "In your book you have to change the statement that the earth moves around the sun, because it goes against the Bible. The Bible says that the sun goes around the earth, and that's everybody's experience, too. Certainly it appears so. In the morning it rises, in the evening it goes down—it looks as if it is going around the earth.

Galileo was seventy-five years old—he was almost dragged from his deathbed to the court to give an apology, because anything that is said in the Bible cannot be disbelieved. It is the word of God; no enquiry is possible. Galileo said, "Such a small thing, which has nothing to do with religion at all...what does it matter whether the sun moves around the earth or the earth moves around the sun? It has no religious significance."

The pope said, "It is not a question of religious significance. The question is that if one thing is wrong in the Bible then the faith is shaken—perhaps other things may be also wrong. If God has some stupid idea, then what is the guarantee that other things that are said are not of the same quality? So not a single word can be questioned."

Galileo must have been a man with a great sense of humor. He said, "To me it makes no difference. I will change it in the book, I will write that the sun moves around the earth, but my statement will not make any difference at all. The earth will go on moving around the sun, in spite of my statement. How can my statement make any difference to the earth?" And that's what he did. He changed his statement and in a note, a footnote, he wrote: "It makes no difference to the earth or to the sun—they go on their way. I am changing it because I don't want to be unnecessarily harassed in my old age."

And it has been so continually since Galileo: everything that science comes to discover goes against the Bible; again and again the same problem arises.

Because science has been progressing in the West, the struggle has been between science and Christianity. But if we look, the same question is valid about every religion. Hinduism believes that the earth is flat, not round. But no Hindu makes a point of saying that the idea should be discarded, it goes against our research. In the Hindu scriptures it says that the sun is smaller than the earth, which is absolute nonsense—the sun is sixty thousand times bigger than the earth. But no Hindu even bothers.

And, most fundamentally, in the first place these things should not be in the religious scriptures, because religion has nothing to do with the size of the sun or the size of the earth. We should take out everything that is not religious from the religious scriptures.

Religious scriptures will need, every ten years, a new edition, because science will go on progressing, enquiring. And the way science enquires and progresses is exactly the way of man's inner search. He also doubts, questions, is skeptical, tries to find the truth himself. He becomes a lab unto himself.

Gautam Buddha could not find any God within himself. He searched to the very ultimate core of his being and he found no God. And if God is not existent in human consciousness, then God cannot be existent in the mountains, in the trees, which are far lower.

The people who have come to the idea of God and have been preaching it, how have they found it? Where have they found it, and what is their method of finding it? Nothing is said about it in any scripture—you simply have faith. But why should one have faith in anybody else, who may be lying, who may be disillusioned himself, who may be insane?

I cannot conceive that Moses encountered God, because God is not a person. So if anything happened, it must have been an illusion, it must have been a projection. And projections are very easy. Just go on a three-week fast, and your mind starts losing the capacity to ask questions. Your mind starts coming to a point where you cannot divide what is dream and what is real.

It is just as it happens to small children. They were dreaming of a beautiful toy and they wake up: the toy is not there and they are crying—"Where is my toy?" And you cannot convince them, "You were dreaming, and this is reality. You have changed the whole dimension. That was your fiction, your idea, your mind and your imagination, and this is reality. It has nothing to do with your mind and your imagination."

All the religions have been teaching fasting. Nobody has bothered to ask why all the religions are agreed on fasting. My own understanding is that the reason is that after a certain time of fasting... Your intelligence needs protein to remain functioning. After three weeks the reservoir of protein in your brain is exhausted—then you are again in the state of a child. You don't know what is dream and what is real. It is those moments when people have realized Jesus Christ, Krishna, Gautam Buddha, Mahavira, or whatever has been always conditioned in their mind; it becomes projected. And they don't now have intelligence enough to feel the distinction between the real and the unreal.

The people like Moses or Jesus who have said that they have encountered God face to face must have been in such a state—which can be experimentally created. And things are very clear: a Christian never comes to see Krishna; a Hindu never comes to see Christ because a Hindu mind is not being continuously conditioned to Christ—he sees

Krishna. The Buddhist never sees Krishna, the Jaina never sees Krishna.

You will be surprised that according to Jaina scriptures, Krishna is suffering in the seventh hell because he was the cause of the greatest war India has suffered, of all that violence. And in fact there is some truth in it. Arjuna was not willing to fight. He wanted to retire from fighting, he wanted to go to the Himalayas to meditate. He said, "It is better—the others can keep the throne. Anyway they are my brothers. And what is the point of killing all these people?"—because it was a family struggle and both parties were connected in many ways.

Arjuna's own master, who had made him the best archer in the world, was on the other side because he was also the master of his brothers. Krishna was fighting on the side of Arjuna, and his own army was fighting on the other side because both parties had approached Krishna to join them. He said, "Now this is difficult. I am alone—how can I join two parties? You are both friends so you can choose: I will fight on one side and my army will fight on the other side."

It was a very strange war in which everybody was related. The grandfather of Arjuna, whom he loved and respected, was on the other side. The people with whom he was fighting were his cousin-brothers, he had played and grown up with them. Millions of people would be killed.

And his argument was absolutely valid: "After killing all these people, sitting on a throne built on all these corpses is absolutely meaningless. I will not be happy, I will be miserable my whole life. What will I gain? I won't even have people to celebrate with. Killing my own people with my own hands does not seem worthwhile. It gives me a clear idea that it is better to go to the mountains and to meditate and to forget all about this."

But Krishna persisted. When he could not continue to argue, he brought in the last argument: "It is God's will. Now you cannot disbelieve in God's will, and it is God's will that you should fight."

Now this has been the strategy of all the priests all over the world—"God's will." But I am surprised that a man of the intelligence of Arjuna did not ask, "If you know God's will, why is he not speaking directly to me? If it is God's will, *you* fight. But as far as I am concerned, I feel *this* is God's will, that I get out of this chariot and go to the mountains." In his place, that's what I would have done. "Then that's perfectly good: if that is God's will for you... to me this is God's will. And if I have to choose, I will choose my own rather than choosing yours."

But this idea of faith has been used to simply destroy your arguments, your intelligence, and create fear. If you don't believe in God then there is hell. If you believe, then you have paradise and all the pleasures. The Christian goes on seeing Christ, the Hindu goes on seeing Krishna, the Buddhist goes on seeing Buddha. And to see these people, simple psychological methods have been used: you should continuously pray. That makes you gullible. A man waking up in the morning starts praying to Krishna the first thing— or to Christ; he goes to the church, listens to the priest, reads the Bible or the Gita, which all preach, "Have faith." And it is repeated thousands of times his whole life.

There are people who become monks and move to a monastery—they are the most prone to experience God because twenty-four hours a day they have nothing else to do except go on repeating a certain mantra, a certain name. They become hypnotized with the name, with the figure.

And all the religions teach that fasting purifies you. I don't understand how hunger can purify. If hunger purifies people then why should we try to destroy poverty? We are destroying pure people, spiritual people! We should make everybody hungry! Hunger cannot purify. And look deeply into it: while you are hungry you think that you are not eating, but your body is absorbing your own flesh. That's why you go on losing weight; otherwise where does your weight go?

I have been condemned by Jainas because I said, at their conferences, "To fast is almost equal to meat-eating—and you pretend to be nonviolent people, vegetarians. But fasting means non-vegetarianism—you are eating yourself." A very healthy man can live through a fast of three months; but after three months he will be just a skeleton, and then death is certain because now he has no more reserve to absorb. He cannot absorb bones. But all these people have stopped their following from thinking. I said, "My challenge is based on a simple fact, that you lose weight—I simply ask where your weight goes. You absorb it.

"Your body needs some energy every day. Working, walking, sitting—whatever you are doing, your body needs energy, and food is simply fuel. If you are not giving it fuel, then the body starts eating itself—it has a dual system just for emergency purposes. There may be a time when food is not available, you may be lost in a forest; the body accumulates some flesh for such times." But you cannot raise such questions.

And secondly, if you fast you are depriving your intelligence. There is a hierarchy—just as in every household there is a certain set of priorities, such that if you are hungry you won't purchase a television, you will purchase food, which is a more basic necessity. But if you have enough food you are not going to go on purchasing food. You will start thinking of purchasing something else—better furniture, a better house, a television, or radio or literature or music. You will start, but if suddenly your money is gone then the first things to go will be the higher things. The television will go first, the radio will go. You will retain your basic needs to the very last.

And that's how it happens when you fast. The first attack is on intelligence because that is the highest in you, and not a basic factor—life can exist without it; all the animals exist without it. So your intelligence starts disappearing. If you remain hungry your love, which you have always thought such a great quality, will start disappearing. A hungry man cannot be loving. To a hungry man you cannot give beautiful literature to read, or beautiful music to listen to. That will simply be an ugly joke. He needs food. So if you fast for three weeks—I have fasted, and I talk only about things which I have tried—after three weeks it becomes difficult to figure out whether you are dreaming or whether it is a reality. You just cannot make the distinction. The faculty that used to make the distinction is no longer there.

That is the reason that all the religions insist on fasting. They disagree on everything else, but they don't disagree on basic elements—fasting, praying, continuous chanting, going to the church or the temple or the mosque, remaining absolutely faithful to the holy book—it may be the Koran, it may be the Gita, it may be the Bible, it does not matter.

But if you see, then the basic things are similar and their function is similar.

Gnosticism is a very revolutionary concept, and it never became a mass phenomenon. It always remained a very small stream of chosen people who had dropped all the nonsense the masses had been following, and who had tried on their own to reach into the inner core of their being.

Faith does not change you, you remain the same, but a Gnostic experience transforms you. And that is the only criterion to be used—whether your knowledge is true or your knowledge is borrowed, whether it changes you or it simply becomes accumulated in your memory. You can become a good teacher, a good priest, a good leader, but you cannot become a good human being.

It happened that just in the last part of the nineteenth century, Rani Rasmani built a temple in Calcutta, in Dakshineshwar on the bank of the Ganges. But Rani Rasmani was not a high-caste Hindu, she was a sudra, she was untouchable. So no Brahmin was ready to worship in her temple, although she was immensely rich and she was ready to give as much money as you wanted. She explained to the Brahmins, "I have not even entered the temple; I simply go up to the steps and bow down from there. I have not entered the inner shrine; I have not even seen the statue of Krishna that is inside the temple. It is made with my money, but money cannot be sudra because money is continuously changing hands from sudra to Brahmin, from Brahmin to *chhatriya*. So you cannot call the temple a sudra temple." But no Brahmin was ready to be a priest in her temple—all over Bengal she searched.

Ramakrishna agreed. He was uneducated. There are only two classes of Bengali, and he was very poor. The whole village tried to prevent him, but they all knew he was a little eccentric: if he decides something, then he decides.

They talked much about it, that it was built by a sudra. He said, "All the temples are made by sudras because the labor, the craftsmen—they all belong to the sudra. Every temple is made by sudras. Can you show me a temple which is made by Brahmins?" Not only are they made by sudras, but the most beautiful parts are made by Mohammedans, because they have a traditional craftsmanship in marble. What they can do nobody else can do. So Ramakrishna said, "All temples are made by sudras, there is no question about it. And money does not matter—money goes on moving. I cannot refuse her, because it is a question of Krishna being there, unworshipped. You have made Krishna also a sudra, an untouchable! The rani herself cannot enter. I am going."

He went. The rani was happy, but on alert because the man looked a little eccentric. But someone was better than no one, so she accepted Ramakrishna. And then complaints started coming about him. The complaints were that sometimes he fights with Krishna. Rather than worshipping him, he shouts at him, fights with him. He uses vulgar language before him—Ramakrishna came from a village. Sometimes just to punish Krishna, he does not give him food. And sometimes he dances the whole day from morning to evening, praying to Krishna. The rani asked Ramakrishna, "What is going on?"

He said, "Everything is going well. When he is good to me I am good to him, and when he is nasty to me I am nasty to him. Sometimes I am praying for hours and he does not appear; then I punish him the next day: I don't give him food. That brings him to his senses. Certainly, I also don't eat that day. I cry the whole day because I have not given food to him, I have not even opened the door—I have let it remain locked."

One experience of Ramakrishna will show you how illusions can be created. In the beginning—it was the birthday of Krishna—he told him, "You have to appear today. It is no ordinary day, it is your birthday. I will dance and sing the whole day and the whole night. And if you don't appear"—a sword used to hang there in the temple—he said, "I will take the sword and cut off my head."

He danced the whole day; the evening came, the night came. It was in the middle of the night—everything was silent. The temple is in a lonely place on the Ganges. Hungry the whole day, dancing the whole day, tired, utterly tired, he was continuously singing and praying, "Appear to me!" Then he pulled out the sword and was going to cut off his head when, at that moment, Krishna appeared. The sword fell from Ramakrishna's hand when he saw Krishna.

Now, it is so simple—a psychological matter. If you do such things you lose the balance of your mind. And Ramakrishna was childish in his behavior, in his living. He was praised as a saint because he was childlike, but because he was childlike he was experiencing Krishna face to face.

One of the great masters was passing through India.... There is a tradition of many masters: they go around the Ganges, all the way to the source, and then back along the other bank to where it falls into the ocean. One master was simply passing by and he came to know about Ramakrishna, and heard that he sees Krishna. He laughed. He said, "The man must be innocent but gullible. He must be innocent but childlike."

He remained in the temple; he talked to Ramakrishna. He explained to him what was happening: "What you are doing is all your creation. It is your imagination. Rama does not appear to you, Vishnu does not appear to you, Shiva does not appear to you. There is no question of Christ and Moses and others. Why does only Krishna appear to you? It is your imagination. And if you put so much pressure on your mind that you are going to cut off your head, naturally the mind is going to do anything to save your life."

Ramakrishna said, "Then you help me to get rid of this illusion."

The master said, "I can help, but the real thing has to be done by you. You sit silently, close your eyes, and when Krishna appears before your eyes, just cut him into two pieces and he will fall apart. There is nothing in it."

Ramakrishna asked, "From where do I bring a sword to cut him?"

And the master said, "From wherever you have brought this Krishna! If you can bring Krishna, from the same imagination you can bring a sword and cut him in two."

Ramakrishna tried three or four times, but the moment he saw Krishna he would start swaying and he would forget the sword and the cutting, and the master and all his teaching. The master said, "You are impossible! I am wasting my time. When you see Krishna appear in your mind you don't cut him; rather, you start swaying. And I can see on your face that you are enjoying the experience."

Ramakrishna said, "I know that I am wasting your time, but what am I to do, because when he appears I simply forget myself."

So the master said, "I will bring a piece of glass, and when I see that you have started swaying and your face is looking ecstatic, I will cut exactly in the middle of your forehead with the glass to remind you that this is the time. You do the same: take the sword and cut Krishna in two."

He actually cut the forehead of Ramakrishna, and Ramakrishna gathered courage and cut Krishna inside. He remained for six hours in absolute silence, and when he opened his eyes, his first words were, "The last barrier has fallen... the last barrier has fallen."

Our own imagination is our last barrier. Once we are without imagination, then reality is there face to face. It is not Christian, it is not Hindu, it is not Mohammedan.

Gnosticism simply says this much: each individual should follow his own inner being, dropping thoughts, imagination, emotions, sentiments, anything that comes in the way. It is not you. The simple principle of Gnosticism is that anything that you can see as an object is not you. You are the seer, so you cannot be the seen. "I can see the furniture, then I am not the furniture. Whatever I can see, I am not it."

So go on dropping all that you can see inside yourself until you come to a space where you cannot see anything. Just the seer remains in its utter purity, innocence. And that is the moment of a great revolution—perhaps the only revolution there is, because the seer cannot see anything, there is nothing to obstruct it.

That is the meaning of the word *object*. Object means "that which obstructs you." There is no object there—all is empty. It can go as far as... but there is nothing. Then it turns upon itself, then it becomes its own object. When the subject itself becomes its own object—in other words, when the observer is the observed, too, when the knower is the known, too—you have arrived home. That is the meaning of Gnosticism.

There is a certain relationship between anarchism and Gnosticism because both depend on the individual. And anarchism will be impossible without Gnosticism, because only Gnosticism can transform people and can bring such quality and energy in them that they don't need any government at all.

A man of awareness does not need anybody else to tell him what to do, what not to do. He does not need the moral teacher, the priest, the policeman, the judge. They all become meaningless. And it will be one of the greatest days in the history of man when government becomes useless and is to be dropped. That means man has transcended all animality in him—violence, anger, hatred—all that needs a government to control people; otherwise there will be so many rapes, and there will be so many murders. There will be so many thefts, and nobody will be safe.

The government is simply an agreement of the society. "We are not capable of controlling ourselves—we need a central control, powerful enough so that individuals cannot dare... or if they dare to do something, then they can be punished."

Even with the government, crime goes on growing, the jails go on growing, the judges go on growing, the criminals go on growing, the laws go on growing. So if you simply remove the government, there will be chaos, and all that is repressed in man out of fear... because both government and religion, the two powerful institutions, use fear and greed to repress your animal. They don't change it. If you are caught, the government will send you to jail to be punished. If you are not caught, then the religions will send you to hell to suffer. It is a basic agreement that if your action is found out, it becomes a crime; if it is not found out, it remains a sin. But on both bases the fear is there that you will have to suffer.

And on the other hand, if you remain good the government has rewards. You become a Nobel Prize winner, and so many awards around the world for people who have proved themselves to be good, who have repressed everything that can be objectionable—they are rewarded. And if they are not rewarded here, they will be rewarded in paradise with all the pleasures of the world. But this is only a strategy to keep man's animality somehow repressed. It does not bring any change.

Gnosticism means a change in your very being.

Then you don't need any fear; you don't need any hell, and you don't need any awards. You don't need any heaven, because to transcend your animality is the greatest reward possible. It is so blissful and so ecstatic to become really human that there is no need for anything else to be added to it. So Gnosticism has no God, has no heaven, no hell—those are religious types of government.

So I can see a relationship between anarchism and Gnosticism. But Gnosticism is more fundamental, has to happen first; only then can anarchism have a chance. Up to now it has remained a utopia.

Fourteen

The Only Hope Left – Our Will to Live

Osho,

Why is it that so many people abandon their intelligence, their sensitivity, their responsibility and their individuality when they become part of a group? Must the rebellious spirit always be alone?

The rebellious spirit is basically the experience of one's own individuality, absolutely free from any kind of psychological slavery. It is a revolt against being reduced to a cog in the wheel; it is against the crowd mind. The crowd mind is the lowest mind in existence. It is the minimum sensibility, minimum consciousness, minimum love, minimum life. One simply survives, one does not live, because life is not a dance.

The crowd never wants anybody to be unique—it hurts the crowd mind. The unique person is a humiliation because it reminds people of what they are and what they could have been. The presence of the unique person makes them aware of what they have missed—and they have missed their whole life. They cannot forgive the unique person, although he has done no harm to them. He has always done great service to humanity: he has brought more beauty to existence, more poetry to life, has created more songs in the soul—he is the very salt of the earth.

All that man is, whatsoever is great in man, belongs to only a very few unique individuals' contribution. But the crowd cannot forgive them. It can forgive criminals, it can forgive murderers, it can forgive politicians, it can forgive any kind of person in the world, but it cannot forgive a man who has an individuality of his own, who is not part of the collective mind.

It reminds me of the crucifixion of Jesus. The man was absolutely harmless. He had not done anything wrong to anybody, he was not a criminal. And the governor general of Judea was Roman, he was not a Jew. Judea was under the Roman Empire, and every year at the annual festival of the Jews they were allowed to forgive one person from all those who were going to be murdered on that day. On that day it was decided, for all the criminals who had been sentenced to death. Millions of people gathered in Jerusalem and it was a great entertainment to see people crucified—such is the barbarous instinct in the crowd.

Governor General Pontius Pilate was perfectly aware that this young man, Jesus, was not a criminal. But the whole crowd of the Jews, their priests, the high priest, were unanimously asking that he should be crucified. He tried to persuade the priests, but they were absolutely deaf to any persuasion. Finally Pontius Pilate talked to Jesus and felt immensely sorry for the young man. Jesus was only thirty-three, he had not seen more than thirty-three springs in his life, and it was absolutely unjust.

But Pontius Pilate was a politician—and the politician knows nothing about justice or injustice, right or wrong; he always thinks in terms of power. Everything is decided to help him to be in power. He was afraid that if he refused to crucify this young, harmless, innocent person, his political career would be jeopardized. All the Jews would appeal to the Roman emperor that Pilate should be removed from Judea. His whole career, respect, power, richness—in Judea he was almost a king—were at risk. But still he tried his best; he talked with Jesus and he became even more convinced that Jesus was innocent.

There was only one hope—because there were two other criminals to be crucified with Jesus Christ: he would ask the crowd, "Whom do you want to be forgiven?" And he hoped that for their own son, utterly innocent, they would come to their senses and would ask that his life should be saved. In comparison to Jesus the other two were as criminal as could be. One had committed three murders, a few rapes; the other had committed seven murders, was a drunkard, was a nuisance. He had been in the jail almost his whole life. He would come out and within two or three days he was bound to do something and he would be back again—jail was his home.

His name was Barabbas, and when Pontius Pilate asked the crowd, "Whom do you want to be released on this religious festival, your festival, your national festival?"—with one voice, the crowd shouted, "Barabbas, we want Barabbas back." Even Barabbas could not believe it. Looking at this young man... he had heard about Jesus that he was absolutely innocent. Even Barabbas felt ashamed and guilty that he was being saved. And these idiots who were shouting his name—he had harassed them his whole life! But he was saved and Pontius Pilate, just out of frustration, went inside and washed his hands.

His washing of the hands had remained without any commentary until Sigmund Freud, almost two thousand years later. Why did he wash his hands? Sigmund Freud, who was always looking deeper into symbols, said that whenever people feel that they have done whatever they could do, then they wash their hands of it completely; they are no more a part of it. He was not responsible for the crucifixion of an innocent and harmless person. But why was the crowd so against Jesus and not against Barabbas?—because after his release, just the third day, Barabbas murdered again and was back in jail.

The psychology of the crowd has to be understood. You are asking, "Why is it that so many people abandon their intelligence, their sensitivity, their responsibility and their individuality, when they become part of a group?"

When you become part of a group, a crowd, a mass, a collectivity, you surrender yourself; you say, "Now the group exists, I am no more." As an individual, you have committed suicide. Now you will think the way the group thinks, you will live the way the group lives. You will be obedient, subservient, a perfect slave, because the more you are a perfect slave the more respect you will gain from the crowd, from the group, from the collectivity you have become a part of. The collectivity honors those who sacrifice themselves.

Yes, your ego will be fulfilled. It is to fulfill your ego that you sacrifice everything—your intelligence, your sensitivity, your responsibility, your individuality—and just become a mechanical part which cannot say no to anything.

The rebel has to remain an individual. That does not mean that he cannot be friendly with others, that he cannot love others, that he cannot join people. But he loves without losing his individuality, without losing his freedom. He can become part of a group, making it clear to the group that "I am not surrendering to you or anybody. I am just joining you with my individuality intact, my intelligence free, my individuality undamaged. I will respect you and I expect the same from you; neither are you my slave nor am I your slave—we are friends." But such groups have not existed up to now.

This is my dream, this is my hope, because all groups—religious, political, social—have been against the individual. I would like communes in the world that are not against the individual, but are a support and a nourishment to the individual. The group in itself has no soul; the soul belongs to the individual. The group exists for the individual, not vice versa. The individual does not exist for the group.

But up to now, this has been the rule: if you are a Christian, then you exist for Christianity—Christianity does not exist for you. If you are a Hindu, then you exist for Hinduism, and if there is a need to die, you will have to die for Hinduism. But Hinduism is neither living for you nor dying for you. Just words, ideologies, fictions, have destroyed the reality. The individual is the only reality, the very crown of existence, the highest peak that existence has been able to reach up to now.

Hence, I teach the rebel. That does not mean that the rebels will not have their friends, that they will not live in communes, that they will all be solitary, living in caves in the Himalayas absolutely alone—that is not my intention at all. I want to change the structure. The society should be for the individual; then there is nothing harmful in it. It should be a help, a nourishing ground for growth, for intelligence, for consciousness, for sensitivity; and it will allow enough space, enough territory to every individual.

The past has been utterly ugly. Even in small relationships, even in families, the individual is crushed. Even two persons getting married, and their individualities are in danger. Their intelligences are in danger. We have become so accustomed, through thousands of years, to possessing each other. Freedom is only a beautiful word. Poets sing songs of it, dreamers dream about it, but reality is simply a sick slavery.

> Tom was thinking about getting married, so he wrote to his father for some advice. His father wrote back: "I can't tell you how happy I am to hear about your impending marriage. You will find marriage the most wonderful state of bliss and happiness.
>
> "As I look across the table at your dear mother, I realize with great pride how full and wonderful our years together have been. By all means, get married. You have our blessings. It will be the happiest day of your life... Sincerely, Dad.
>
> "P.S. Your mother just left the room—stay single, you idiot."

This is how things are. Everybody is trying to enslave everybody else; and in slavery, naturally, a few things which are very delicate start dying: intelligence, sensitivity, responsibility, individuality. And marriage is the smallest group, only two persons. Then the groups go on becoming bigger and bigger; the bigger the group, the more you are lost.

And then there are nations, great religions—there are seven hundred million Catholics. Once you become a Catholic—or, unfortunately, you may have been born a Catholic—you don't have any scope, any space to expand. From everywhere your wings are cut, you are kept reduced in every possible way. Because if you are allowed freedom, there is a danger you may not be Catholic at all. You may even go against Catholicism....

A small boy in a school was crying and his teacher asked him, "What is the matter, Johnny? You have never cried like that. Has somebody died?"

He said, "It is worse than that. My dog has given birth to seven small puppies, and when I asked those puppies, 'Are you Catholics?' they all waved their heads, so I was feeling very happy."

The teacher said, "Then why you are weeping?"

He said, "Today, their eyes opened, and when I asked, 'Are you Catholics?' they started looking at each other, they didn't answer at all."

You have to be blind to be a Catholic, to be a Mohammedan, to be a Hindu, to be a Buddhist. If your eyes open, it becomes impossible for you to remain confined to superstitions, lies of all kinds, and to go on believing in fictions when your intelligence raises doubts. Your church demands of you, never to doubt—that is the greatest sin.

But intelligence never grows without doubting, without questioning. It is the natural growth of intelligence to question. Just to believe means the intelligence need not grow—for what and why? There is nothing to seek and nothing to search for, you simply have faith in the priest and keep your eyes closed.

This has been so, but this need not be so forever. And those who understand me clearly can see it happening here already. Nobody is dictating anything to you, nobody is giving you any discipline, nobody is telling you what is right and what is wrong. Because of this, I am condemned all over the world. Perhaps no man has been condemned so aggressively, so violently, and on such a large scale. And what is my crime? My crime is that I am trying to create groups where people are individual, intelligent seekers, meditators, lovers. Not believers, not faithful to any holy scripture, not faithful to any dead prophet—trusting only their own intelligence and their own still, small voice, heard in the silences of the heart, in deep meditation.

Who am I to give you a moral code? You have to find your morality yourself, and only the morality that you have found for yourself will give you dignity. It will not be a bondage, you will not feel burdened, enslaved, imprisoned. On the contrary, you will feel integrated, crystallized, more pure and more clear. You are living according to your own light, and the more you use your light, your intelligence, your silence, the more it grows. Remember always, if you stop using anything it dies. Don't use your eyes for a few years and then you will not be able to see.

Just here in Pune, a few years ago, there was a very beautiful man, Meher Baba. He had remained silent for perhaps more than fifty years. He had taken a vow of silence for only three years in the beginning, but then he enjoyed the silence so much that he continued for three more years. But after three years, if you continue to be silent... three years is the limit. After three years, if you continue, then your vocal chords start dying. Unused, any machine, any mechanism becomes just junk.

Then he became world famous, and people began asking him to start speaking. He would promise, "From the coming birthday, I am going to speak." This he declared almost twenty times; and each year, when the day came to speak, he didn't speak. People wondered, what is the reason, why has he not fulfilled his promise? He is a man of truth. But nobody thought of a simple thing....

When I used to travel around the country, his private secretary, Adi Irani, used to come to see me while I was visiting Ahmed Nagar. That is where Meher Baba used to live most of the time. He had a place in Pune also, but most of the time he was in Ahmed Nagar. Whenever I used to go to Ahmed Nagar, Adi Irani would tell me many things about Meher Baba, and asked many questions. He asked me why he was not speaking—there was so much contemplation about it going on among the disciples.

I said, "It is nothing to contemplate, he has remained too long in silence. He tries, he makes an effort—that's why he goes on promising—but the mechanism has failed. And I can say to you," I told Adi Irani, "that he will never speak. Not that he is lying—he is trying hard; he will try up to his last breath to manage to speak. But how can you speak if your mechanism of speaking is nonfunctioning?"

Adi Irani said, "This is strange, none of us has ever thought about it. But perhaps you are right." And that's what happened... Meher Baba never spoke, and until his death he continued to promise, but he could not do anything.

If you don't use your intelligence—and every religion wants you not to use your intelligence... their strategy is that you should believe, have faith. They don't say directly, "Don't use your intelligence;" but in an indirect and in a cunning way they stop you from using intelligence. If you have faith there is no need for intelligence. If you have beliefs there is no need for intelligence; and a man who has become retarded because of beliefs and faith cannot be sensitive.

Sensitivity needs great intelligence. The higher your intelligence, the more sensitive you are. Buffalos are not sensitive, neither are donkeys; it needs intelligence to be sensitive. But no religion wants you to be sensitive, they are all afraid of your becoming a power unto yourself. A sensitive person becomes a power, a tremendous powerhouse. He has his own intelligence, he has his own love, he has his own insight into things. He has clarity of vision, he has an aesthetic sense for beauty—all these things are dangerous.

The wife does not want the husband to be sensitive toward beauty, because that is a danger. There are so many beautiful women; it is better that all sensitivity for beauty is completely crushed. Then the husband remains henpecked forever. In the same way, no husband wants his wife to be sensitive about beauty because there are so many men, and the wife, if her heart is still alive and beats, and if she can still feel the spring... there is danger. She can fall in love with somebody and it is beyond your power. If you fall in love, you cannot do anything, you are simply helpless.

The group demands that you kill yourself and just survive—don't live. Just survive enough so that you can be used as laborers, as clerks, as police commissioners, as presidents, as prime ministers... but just survival, not more than that. Living totally, intensely, burning your torch of life from both sides together, you become a tremendous danger to the crowd. Because everybody starts feeling he could also have lived the way you are living—this dance could have been his, too, this song could have been his, too. And because you remind him about the wounds that he is carrying and hiding within himself, because you make him utterly nude and exposed to himself, he cannot forgive you.

Socrates and Jesus and al-Hillaj Mansoor and Sarmad—these beautiful people, these individuals who had not become part of any group, any society, who remained like solitary cedars of Lebanon high in the sky, alone, almost touching the stars... They created jealousy in people, fear in people, and most importantly they opened their closed wounds. It hurts, it hurts so badly that it is better to remove these people so that millions who have lost their souls, who have sold themselves in the market place, can be at ease again.

The reason for crippling the individual in the past is very clear. But the future has not to repeat the past. The future has to bring a new dawn to man's consciousness. Individuals can live together, share their love, share their joy, share their wisdom; but there is no need to possess anybody, not even your own children. You don't have any right to possess them. They come through you but you are not their owners.

There is no need of any marriage—these are the ugly institutions created by the collective mind. There is no need of any nations. With the disappearance of the nations, wars will disappear automatically. There is no need for organized religions because religion is a private phenomenon. It is nobody's business to interfere into my religion.

And my religion does not belong to a tradition. Those who belong to a tradition don't have a religion, they only have a belief system. They have not found any truth by their own efforts, they have not created anything that they can call their own contribution to existence. They don't have any right for prayer. The existence has been giving you life and all that life implies—its gifts are immeasurable. And if you cannot contribute anything creatively, all your prayers are just deceptions. There is no God to listen to them, you are talking to yourself.

If people start talking to themselves you call them mad, but if they say they are doing prayer you call them great saints, religious people. These are also mad because there is no God, no evidence, no proof. It is better if they start talking to the trees—at least there is someone. But they raise their eyes towards the sky, hoping that, sitting on a golden throne, God is listening. For millions and millions of years listening to your prayers... either he must have gone mad and jumped out of his golden throne and committed suicide, or he must have become frozen, a fossil. Nobody's prayer is ever heard and nobody's prayer is ever answered—all your prayers are monologues.

But society has been playing with individuals in such inhuman ways that even madness is praised if it is helpful to keep people in control. All the morality—also called "religious discipline"—is nothing but to keep people in control. I want you to be in your own control, to take responsibility in your own hands. Be alert and aware, and out of your awareness will come all your relatedness, friendships, loves, societies, communes; but there is no need for anybody to sacrifice.

> Hymie Goldberg rang his wife from his office: "I would like to bring Cohen home to dinner tonight," he told her.
>
> "To dinner tonight?" she screamed. "You idiot, you know that the cook has just left, I have got a cold, the baby is cutting his teeth, the furnace is broken and the butcher won't give us any more credit until we pay up."
>
> "I know, I know," Goldberg interrupted quietly. "That's why I want to bring him—just to see the

whole scene. The poor fool is thinking of getting married."

All our relationships have become poisonous, and a great revolution is needed to change all this garbage of centuries that has collected around our beings. But it is possible—not only possible, it has to happen, because there is a limit to everything; this insanity that we have lived with for thousands of years has come to the peak. Because of this madness, we have created nuclear weapons, knowing well that if any war happens it will be the destruction of all. Nobody will be defeated, nobody will be victorious. Still, nations go on creating nuclear weapons. Even poor nations, which are not able to feed their people, want to join the race, want to put billions of dollars into destructive war material.

Almost half of India's people are hungry; they go to sleep with no food in their stomachs. If they can manage one meal a day they are fortunate. Yet, India is ready to sell wheat to purchase more of the materials necessary for creating atomic energy, nuclear weapons, and being ready for a third world war. It is not a question of some individual gone mad, it is the whole humanity which has gone crazy. This is the very limit, unbearable. Either we have to commit suicide because of all these idiots who are creating the situation for a global murder, or we have to change the whole past: its institutions, its education, its ways of living, its ways of being religious. Unless we are ready for a total revolution, man cannot be saved.

My hope is that howsoever far man may have gone crazy, he still wants to live. His will to live is the only hope left. We have to put more fire into the will to live. We have to create wildfires around the world—for more life, for more love, for more songs, for more music—so that it becomes impossible for humanity to go along with these political, scientific, and other kinds of madmen to commit suicide. It all depends on the vast humanity in the world. If they simply say, "We have decided to live and we have decided to make this world more beautiful, and we have decided to dissolve nations so that we can dissolve wars, and we have decided to dissolve religions because they are also causes of war and discrimination..." Unless such a miracle happens, man's history has come to its last chapter.

Fifteen

Anarchism and Consciousness

Osho,

What is the difference between the individual anarchism of Bakunin and the rebel of your vision?

I love Bakunin and his philosophy of anarchism, but he is an impractical, unpragmatic philosopher. He simply goes on praising the beauties of anarchism: no government, no armies, no police, no courts. And I absolutely agree with him. But he had no idea and no plan for how this dream could be made into a reality.

Looking at man, you will need the government; looking at man, you will need the police. Otherwise there will be a multiplication of murders, rapes, thefts... life will be a chaos. Anarchism would not come, only a chaos. People would start making gangs, those gangs would exploit the weaker people and life would not become better, it would become worse.

Bakunin's anarchism is a utopia, a great dream. I don't talk about anarchism. My own understanding is if we can transform man, if we can bring more and more people to meditation, if we can make more and more people unrepressed, living an authentic, natural life, sharing their love, having a great compassion for everything living, a reverence for life itself....

These individual revolutionaries, these individual rebels are not just political rebels, they are also rebelling against all the past conditionings. Mostly they are religious rebels; they are finding their own center of being. There are more and more people who are becoming individuals who can rejoice, and who are not going to betray the earth; who are not in favor of any unnatural way of life preached by all the religions. If these individuals spread around the world like a wildfire, then anarchism will be a by-product, not the goal.

For Bakunin it is the goal. He hates governments so much—and he is perfectly right in his hate, because governments have been doing so much harm to the individuality of people. He is against all laws, courts and judges, because these are not to protect justice, not to protect the weak, not to protect the victim—they are there to protect the power, the establishment, the rich. Behind the name of justice, they are enacting a tremendous conspiracy against man.

And Bakunin has no idea why men become rapists, he is not a psychologist. He is a great philosopher of anarchism. The future will owe tremendous respect to people like Bakunin, Bukharin, Tolstoy, Camus, because although they were not very scientific thinkers at least they created the idea. Without providing the foundation, they started talking about the temple.

My whole effort is not to bother about the temple but to make a great foundation; then, to raise the temple is not difficult. Anarchism will be a by-product of a society which is free from religions and religious superstitions; which is psychologically healthy, non-repressive, which is spiritually healthy, not schizophrenic, which knows the beauties of the outside world and also the inner treasures of consciousness, awareness. Unless these people exist first, anarchism is not possible; it can come only as a by-product.

In America, they are so afraid of the anarchist that when they interviewed me for my immigration there, there was a question that I should commit, in writing, that I am not an anarchist. I said to the man who was doing the interview, "I am not an anarchist of the category of Bakunin, Bukharin and Tolstoy, but I have my own anarchism. And you need not be afraid about it, because anarchism is not my goal; my goal is to create individual rebels."

The idea of rebellion is not new, but the idea of rebellion combined with enlightenment is absolutely new—it is my contribution. And if we can make the majority of humanity more conscious, more aware, with a few individuals reaching to the highest peak of enlightenment, then their rebellion will bring anarchism just like a shadow, following on its own accord.

Sixteen

Compromise is your Dignity on the Gallows

Osho,

How can one remain in society, and yet live authentically?

You can be a rebel even in a society which wants you to be part of the establishment. Don't compromise. Even life itself is a lesser value than your individuality and your rebelliousness.

Your rebelliousness is your very spirit.

You are truly a human being only when you are rebellious, when you can say no to anything that goes against freedom, that goes against man's dignity. When you are ready to go to the gallows without any grudge, because you are sacrificing yourself for something far greater and more beautiful—for freedom, for individuality, for expression, for creativity; you are sowing seeds for future generations. You will not be sad, you will be immensely happy that you have not been forced to become a slave, that rather than being enslaved you preferred the gallows.

Unless in this society a person is ready to choose crucifixion rather than consolations, medals, and Nobel Prizes... only such a person can be a rebel and can be truly spiritual. We hope that one day there will be a society where everybody will be so rebellious.

But rebellion does not mean reaction or destruction; rebellion means your highest flowering of consciousness. Unless rebellion brings enlightenment to you, you cannot save it; you will have to compromise. And to compromise is to lose your self-respect, is to lose your dignity as a human being.

Up to now the society has lived under a false idea that people are free. Nobody is free; there are a thousand and one ways to enslave you. Only very rarely have a few people risked everything and remained individuals even at the risk of death—but they are the very salt of the earth. They are the people who have maintained humanity's evolution. Evolution depends on only a very few people; they can be counted on your ten fingers. Others live a life of middle-class comfort, and for that comfort they sell their souls in the marketplace.

If people are really rebels, not just because of their minds but because of their meditation, then there is no problem. With Gautam Buddha there were ten thousand meditators and there was no establishment. Nobody was higher, nobody was lower; nobody had to be ordered what to do. Even Gautam Buddha has never ordered anyone to do a single thing; he simply shared his vision. It is up to you whether to participate in that vision or not. That is going to be your decision, and that is going to be your responsibility.

Freedom brings responsibility.

Those ten thousand people around Gautam Buddha lived a rebellious life; they renounced society. People think that all the religions of the world have renounced society for the same reasons; that is wrong. Except Gautam Buddha, all other religions have renounced the world to gain something in the other world. It is not renunciation, it is pure business, almost a lottery, because here you lose very small things, and there you get a millionfold reward in paradise. Here you lose a woman who is just a pain in the neck; there you get hundreds of beautiful women who always remain young, who don't perspire, who don't need to use deodorants, who have a natural perfume arising out of their bodies; their age is fixed, they have not gone beyond sixteen. For millions of years they are just sixteen. It is perfectly good to renounce a wife here, who is nothing but a trouble, in the hope of getting beautiful women there.

> I have heard that when Muktananda died, one of his disciples was so devoted to him that he could not live another day—the next day he also died. Naturally, the first thing was to look around for where his great master Muktananda was.
>
> He was very much ashamed to see that he was lying down under a beautiful tree—flowers were showering from the tree and Muktananda was lying down naked with a beautiful woman. As he came closer he said, "My God. He was always against pleasures, but perhaps this must be a reward for his great celibacy." Coming closer he saw that it was nobody other than the great film actress, Marilyn Monroe. He fell to the feet of his master and said, "My master, I always knew you would be greatly rewarded."
>
> Monroe said, "You idiot! You don't understand anything. I am not his reward; he is my punishment!"

People are hoping.... Only Gautam Buddha has not given a hope for the future life to his disciples. He has given them the whole kingdom of the present, not of the future. And their renunciation of the world is not against the world. He is the only one who has renounced the world, and his followers have renounced the world, not against the world but against the establishment of the society. They have created a gathering of rebels with no order, with no system except their own consciousness, their own conscience.

He was working on those people to be deeply meditative. Then there is no need of any establishment. You always do the right thing; you cannot, even if you want to, do the wrong thing. You don't need any supervision, you don't need somebody to keep you within the law. Once you have learned the law of love, then all other laws are of no use to you.

Gautam Buddha pulled them out of society for the simple reason that in society they will have to compromise; their consciousness is not so strong that they can remain without compromise.

I don't want my people to leave the world, because twenty-five centuries have passed since Buddha, and it is time that people should be strong enough in their awareness so they can remain in the society without compromising. Although it is far more difficult, it is a great challenge to live in society and not be part of it, to live in society but not allow society to live in you.

That's my special contribution to the religious experience and to the rebellious human beings. In the past they used to escape from the establishment, but that shows cowardliness, fear. Be in the society and live according to your own consciousness, whatsoever the consequences. It is better to suffer those consequences than to escape and show your fearfulness, because fear cannot allow you to rise to your ultimate height. The society can be used as a fire test of whether your rebellion is just a mind game or it is a spiritual growth. Those who are rebellious because of their spiritual growth don't have to fear that they will become part of established society.

>Moishe Finkelstein, a tailor from a small Ukrainian village, applies for membership of the Russian Communist Party in Kiev.
>
>"Who was Karl Marx?" asks the Commissar.
>
>"Never heard of him," replies Moishe.
>
>"Who was Joseph Vissarionovich Stalin?"
>
>"Never met him," answers Moishe.
>
>"Who was Vladimir Ilyich Lenin?"
>
>"Can't say I recall the name," replies Moishe.
>
>"Mr. Finkelstein, are you taking us for idiots?" asked the irritated Commissar.
>
>"No," replies Moishe, "Do you know Irving Levensky?"
>
>"Never heard of him," replied the Commissar.
>
>"So, do you know Bernie Heikleman?" Moishe asked again.
>
>"No," was the reply.
>
>"So you know Hymie Goldberg?" Moishe asked again.
>
>"I don't know who you are talking about," replied the irritated Commissar.
>
>"Well," says Finkelstein, "that's how it is—you have your friends; I have mine!"

And this is how the compromise goes on happening in everybody's life....

The out-of-work actor came home to find his house in a shambles. Lamps were knocked over in the living room, drapes were torn, and in the bedroom the bedspread was ripped and the sheets torn. On the bed lay his wife, badly beaten and bruised, sobbing her heart out.

"What happened? Who did this to you?" raged the actor.

"I... I fought as long as I could, but he was too strong," wailed the wife. "He... he..."

"Who?" rasped the actor. "Tell me and I'll find him and tear him limb from limb."

"It was your agent," said the wife. "He came while you were out."

"My agent?" the actor brightened. "Tell me, does he have a part for me?"

He has forgotten everything. Out of employment, you cannot fight with your agent.

In life, you go on compromising without knowing, not only with the society but even with your family. Even the people you love demand compromise. Nobody likes the individual; everybody wants to overpower you, to dominate you. The husband wants to dominate the wife; the wife in her own ways tries to dominate the husband. The parents dominate the children; the children also in their own way dominate the parents. It is a constant struggle going on in multiple ways, where nobody is allowed to be just himself, where to be oneself is a crime.

But to accept the challenge and to remain yourself, in spite of all the odds, is a great joy. To keep your individuality intact, undamaged, in a society where everybody is trying to dominate you... I don't think it is good to escape from such a society. In the Himalayas, in deep forests, you may think you are yourself—but that is a false notion, because there is no context in which you can put it to the test.

The society is every moment a test. And here, to be just yourself, not out of arrogance, not out of your egoistic feelings... Those people who are arrogant will have to compromise, because there are more arrogant people. Those who are egoists will find sooner or later somebody else who can crush them.

There are different kinds of powers. People slowly, slowly learn not to stand erect, but they start crawling on the ground. In this society, to remain erect and yourself—without arrogance, without ego, but just out of your silence, just out of your awareness—is a tremendous experience and experiment.

I have lived life the way I wanted; it was difficult but it was immensely rewarding. It gave me the feeling that although society may be powerful, if you have guts no power can enslave you. They can kill you, they can destroy you, but they cannot enslave you. And to be destroyed is not undignified; to be killed is not against your individuality, against your dignity, against your pride. In fact, these sacrifices will make you more and more authentically yourself.

Deep down, if you are a meditator, you know your body can be taken away, but your being cannot even be touched—your immortality is sure. Hence, I am adding to rebelliousness a new phenomenon. There have been meditators, but they escaped from the society, and there have been rebellious people who were destroyed by the society. I am bringing two very great qualities together that the world has not known before: the meeting of rebelliousness and meditativeness, the meeting of rebelliousness and religiousness. To me, rebelliousness and religiousness are two sides of the same coin.

There is no need to be afraid because there is nothing that can be destroyed in you. And that which can be destroyed will be destroyed whether you are in the Himalayas, or hiding in the monasteries. The body is going to be destroyed, so there is no need on the part of the body, on the part of the mind, to be ready to be enslaved. This happens because you are not aware of anything more than the body-mind structure. My effort is to make you aware of your immortality.

Once you have tasted the very source of your life, which is eternal, then nothing can make you do things that are not in tune with your own being. You will say yes only when you feel that this yes is not the yes of a slave but of a person of freedom. You will say no if you see that saying yes will be only falling into slavery. But this is possible only if you become aware of your being.

The old rebels were only intellectually rebellious. My rebel has to be spiritually rebellious, and that makes a tremendous difference. The intellectual rebellion is superficial and can be purchased, but the spiritual rebellion is not a commodity in the market; you have transcended the world.

I don't want you to escape the world, I want you to transcend the world—living in it, going through all the fire because you know nothing can destroy you. This certainty can create a gathering of rebels without any establishment. And if any functional kind of mechanism is needed, that is not a problem. Where there are so many people, something functional will be needed. But remember, it is functional—it does not give you any status; a prime minister or a president of a country are nothing more than functional entities; they have a utility, but they don't have any status.

Real status comes only from your realization of yourself, not by sitting on a golden throne. If people bow down to you, remember they are bowing down to the throne, not to you. Tomorrow somebody else will be there. Yesterday there was somebody else and people were bowing down.

I have heard it happened in Jagannathpuri...

It is one of the Hindu religious cities, and it has a great chariot, very ancient, dedicated to God. *Jagannath* means God, the lord of the world. Once every year, the chariot goes through the streets and millions of people gather. Once it happened that a dog was going ahead of the chariot, and thousands of people were falling on the ground, touching the earth. And the dog said, "Great, I must be someone very special!"

Millions of people, but all your presidents and all your prime ministers are in the same position as the dog. People are respectful towards them, not because of them—once they are out of power, nobody even remembers them.

These so-called powerful people don't have any power. There is only one power, and that comes from within. Any power that comes from outside is not yours. As it has come, it will be taken away. So if you are intelligent you will not think yourself anybody special; you are just functional.

In a society of greater consciousness, more intelligence, government will become just a small functional order, it will not be an enslaving mechanism. On the contrary, it will help individuals to become more sharp in their intelligence, deeper in their meditation, and flowering in their enlightenment with great grace.

Only this kind of evolution in consciousness, which is going to happen... Perhaps we are born in the right age when the transformation is going to happen, because the situation is such that either the whole of humanity will die, or it will have to change. And I don't think anybody wants to die.

The only alternative is to be more conscious, more alert, more alive, more loving—and create a new world with a new man, bring a new dawn to humanity.

Seventeen

Religiousness and Rebelliousness: Two Names for the Same Phenomenon

Osho,

What is the religion of a rebellious spirit?

The rebellious spirit can be religious, but cannot have a religion. And the difference between the two is immense, unbridgeable. To be religious is an experience, just like love. It is an encounter with the totality of existence. It is facing yourself in the mirror of life. It is orgasmic in the sense that you melt and merge with the whole—the earth, the trees, the flowers, the sky, the stars. It is an oceanic experience, the dewdrop slipping from the lotus leaf into the ocean. You can say either the dewdrop has become the ocean, or you can say the ocean has become the dewdrop. It is the greatest experience there is.

But to belong to a religion is not an experience, it is just a belief system in which you have been brought up. It is all borrowed. And remember that truth cannot be borrowed. Either it is yours, or it is not there.

Gautam Buddha may have known the truth, but there is no way to follow him, because to follow means to imitate, to follow means to become a shadow, to follow means to betray yourself. Following is nothing but the effort of trying to be somebody that you are not; and that is not your destiny, either.

Jesus is not a Christian, he is a rebellious spirit; he does not belong to any religion, and that is his crime. Jews could not tolerate him because he had become a stranger to his own people; he had started talking about having a direct contact with the universal spirit.

A religion is a marketplace thing. It is a kind of bureaucracy—you should go through the right channels. You are not even allowed to confess to God directly; you have to confess to the priest and the priest will pray for you. The priest has to always be there as a mediator. Religion is the business of the priest; it has nothing to do with religiousness. It is a profession, pure and simple, of exploiting the ignorance and the helplessness of mankind. It is exploiting the fear of death, the fear of the unknown, the fear of the responsibilities of life. The priest takes care—you have to simply believe in his church, his religion, his god, his holy scripture. To belong to a religion is to belong to all kinds of lies and superstitions. To belong to a religion is to belong to the past—which is dead.

A rebellious spirit has no past. A rebellious spirit has only the present and a vast opening towards the future. Religion, to the religious spirit, is not in the holy scriptures but in the holiness of existence. It is not in the prayer taught by the priests of all kinds of religions, it is in the gratitude that one feels before a sunset, before a sunrise. It is in the gratitude that one feels to be a part of this beautiful and tremendously miraculous existence.

It is a prayer without words, it is a song without sound. It is pure silence. And in that silence existence speaks to you. In that silence you speak to existence, there is a dialogue. No one speaks, no one hears, but there is a transfer of energy. Something transpires within you—perhaps a flame that makes you afire.

Religiousness and rebelliousness are basically names of one experience. But to be a part of an organized religion is to be not really alive, not really in search of truth, not in love with existence. It is a kind of death—although you go on breathing, you go on eating. But all your breathing and all your eating drive you only toward the graveyard. You don't grow up, you only grow old.

Only the rebellious spirit grows up; its longing is to touch the stars. It is not satisfied with the trivia of life. Its contentment is far away; its discontentment is a present reality. The rebellious man has a divine discontent in his heart and a longing to find contentment and peace. He is on a pilgrimage towards that contentment. His whole life is a pilgrimage, always moving closer and closer and closer to the ultimate reality—the realization that releases one from all bondage, all frustration, all misery, all anguish, and allows one to taste freedom, truth, beauty, love and an outburst of creativity in the multidimensions of life.

The rebellious person has a golden touch—whatever he touches becomes gold, it does not matter what. He may play on a bamboo flute and it becomes pure gold, twenty-four carat. He may dance alone under the starry sky, and his dance is more meaningful, more significant than all the paintings in the world, all the statues and all the holy scriptures. His creativity may simply be expressed in his silence. But his silence will not be an ordinary silence, just an absence of noise—his silence will be a positive blossoming of roses in his being. You can experience the fragrance of his silence, it is almost tangible.

The organized religions are all dead; the churches, the temples, the mosques, the synagogues... they are all graveyards of the past. And the sooner we convert them into museums the better, otherwise they are going to kill the whole of humanity. They have already killed too much in every person; they have crippled everybody, poisoned everybody; their destruction is uncountable.

You are asking, "What is the religion of a rebellious spirit?"

Rebellion! Rebellion is the religion of a rebellious spirit—to rebel against all exploitation, to rebel against all discrimination, to rebel against oppression, to rebel against all kinds of spiritual slavery, to rebel against all kinds of superstitions. There is so much to rebel against.

And that is only half of the rebellion, because the other half is to rebel *for*. To rebel against superstition is only half—to rebel *for* the truth, to rebel for freedom, to rebel for love, to rebel for a new humanity, to rebel for a new man, a new society, a new kind of consciousness.

Rebellion has two parts. The negative part is against all that is ugly but has been worshipped for centuries, and the positive part is for all that is beautiful but has been ignored for centuries—not only ignored but crucified, poisoned, murdered. Whenever any individual has tried the authentic religion of rebelliousness, his reward has been crucifixion. Hence I want so many rebellious people in the world that it will be difficult to find people to crucify them.

> Mick had returned to his native town after many years overseas. "I hope," said the parish priest, "that you have been loyal to your faith while you have been away."
>
> "Indeed, Father," said Mick, "I have lied, I fought, I cursed, I robbed and I made love to women; but not for a moment did I forget the religion I was brought up in."

What is the point of all these religions? There are three hundred religions in existence in the world today. There are also millions of murders, suicides, rapes, robberies and continuous warfare, either in this part of the world or in another part of the world. What are these religions doing? And everybody is religious! Nobody is disloyal to his religion; he robs, he murders, he rapes, but he remembers that he is a Christian, that he is a Hindu, that he is a Mohammedan, that he is a believer in God, that he is a follower of Gautam Buddha. What does all this following mean? Sheer deception, not only to others, but to yourself. It is strange—so strange that it is almost unbelievable—that there are three hundred religions in the world and there is no peace, no joy, no celebration, no holiness, no divineness anywhere. All these religions are fake. The rebellious spirit has to get rid of all these religions and create only a quality of religiousness without any adjective—simply religious.

It has always been a problem.... In my whole life I have not been able to vote, for the simple reason that whenever the officers reached me to fill in the form so that I could be a valid voter, there was a clause, "What is your religion?"

I said, "I don't have any religion. I am a religious person."

They said, "But all the clauses have to be filled in."

I said, "Then you can take your form back. I am not so much interested in voting anyway, because it is an unnecessary anxiety when you have to choose between two idiots. Whom to vote for?—whoever you vote for, you are voting for an idiot. It is better not to vote, at least your hands are clean. You can see: my hands are absolutely clean!"

Man's problems have increased as time has passed. It should have been otherwise—that the problems would be less and less as man has become more and more cultured, educated, civilized. But the more he is cultured, the more he is civilized, the more he is educated, his problems have increased out of all proportion. And religions go on proclaiming that they have the cure for every disease, for every spiritual sickness. But man is suffering from spiritual sickness all over the world—everybody is feeling hollow. And these religions have not been of any help; on the contrary, they have increased the problems with their wrong, unnatural, stupid teachings.

It was Mrs. Levy's third visit to the doctor for a cure from her cold. "Doctor," she complained, "nothing you have given me has been of any use. Mr. Levy complains that I keep him awake all night with my cough. Can you do something—anything to cure me?"

> "Okay," the doctor replied, "go home and have a hot bath and without drying yourself stand in the nude where there is a strong draft."
>
> "Really," Mrs. Levy sniffed, "will that cure me?"
>
> "No," replied the doctor, "but it will give you pneumonia, and I can cure pneumonia."

These religions have been giving you bigger diseases. Perhaps, in a certain way, when you have a bigger disease you tend to forget the smaller one.

> I have heard about Mulla Nasruddin that he was purchasing shoes in a shop. The shopkeeper said, "Mulla, are you mad or something, because you are trying on shoes that are not going to fit. You need shoes that are one size bigger."

Mulla said, "Don't disturb me. I have always used that size and I am going to continue to use that size. I am a man of principles."

The shopkeeper said, "It is up to you, but you will suffer the whole day. The shoes will pinch you."

Mulla said, "That's what I want."

The shopkeeper said, "But why do you want that?"

He said, "You don't understand the psychology of it. Suffering the whole day, when I come home and take off my shoes, it is such a relief that I say, 'My God!'—it brings such pleasure. Without these shoes, life is nothing but misery. The whole day the shoes keep me away from all miseries because I don't have enough energy to look at other miseries. What my wife is saying, who has ears to hear her? My shoes are pinching me so badly that I am only hearing my shoes. She goes on talking to herself—she has become accustomed to monologues.

"Business is bad, things are going from bad to worse, but nothing worries me. My only worry is my shoes. The shoes keep me away from all the miseries of the world and in the end, before going to bed, taking them off gives me such relief that I sleep so relaxedly, so deeply.... And you are suggesting that I wear shoes that are one size bigger? You are going to destroy my life!"

These religions have provided you all with shoes that don't fit—shoes which may have fit somebody five thousand years ago. They have given you pants which don't fit. They are making a mockery of you, because those shoes are not made according to your needs, those pants are not made for you, those shirts are not made for you. Everything that these religions are supplying for you has been made by somebody else, for somebody else, far back—centuries ago. Nothing fits; everything gives nothing but pain.

But these religions have been teaching you, "Blessed are those who suffer, blessed are those who live in misery, blessed are those whose lives are of hostility, asceticism, self-torture, because they shall inherit the kingdom of God." So just to inherit the kingdom of God you go on wearing shoes that don't fit, caps that are so loose that you cannot see because they cover your eyes. Clothes that are either so small that you want to jump out of them, or so loose that a crowd can live inside them—the whole family can be accommodated.

The rebellious person cannot accept any of this idiocy. His religion is his intelligence. His religion is his consciousness. His religion is his awareness. And out of his awareness, he becomes as free as a bird on the wing, as beautiful as a lotus in the pond, and as joyous as a cuckoo singing from the mango grove. He starts living for the first time, and he knows that life is the only God there is—there is no other God. The rebellious man is a pagan. He worships the trees, he worships the stars, the rivers, the mountains. He worships human beings, he worships everything that is alive—because wherever there is life, there is godliness.

Eighteen

Meditation is the Only Unselfish Act

Osho,

When they become aware that I meditate, some of my friends and family have asked me, "Why are you wasting your time sitting and doing nothing? Wouldn't it be better to spend your time doing virtuous acts like trying to help others? What you call meditation is just selfishness." What is your answer to this type of question?

It has many implications to be understood.

First, in one's unconsciousness one cannot do any virtuous act. Virtue comes out of deep meditation. Virtue is a flower of your realization that you are eternal, immortal, that you are divine. Sharing that divineness is virtue. There is no other virtue in existence.

But all the religions, particularly Christianity, go on emphasizing, "Do virtuous acts. Don't sit silently, it is selfish."

I have to ask, first: when you succeed as a rich man nobody says to you that it is selfish. Everybody praises you: that is great. When you succeed as a politician and become a president or a prime minister nobody says it is selfish, everybody praises you. Success is not selfish—do you see the point?—being super-rich is not selfish, creating materials for destruction of the world is not selfish, accumulating nuclear weapons is not selfish ....

And what is your virtue? Is it unmotivated? Are you not being virtuous—doing service to the poor, or the sick, or the orphans—in order to get into paradise with all its pleasures? It is simply business. Who says it is virtue?

I am reminded of an ancient Chinese parable ....

Every year a festival used to happen in the capital of China. Millions of people would gather—the fair lasted for one month—and even the emperor used to come to inaugurate it. But in those days, in China, the water wells were not protected by walls. In darkness one could easily fall into a well, because there was no wall as a protection.

A man fell into a well. It was getting dark and his eyesight was not good, he was almost blind. He shouted for help, but with millions of people there was so much noise...who was going to hear him?

A Confucian monk passed by and he heard the man asking for help, to be taken out of the well. The Confucian monk said to him, "Don't be worried. Our master, Confucius, has written in his books that every well should have walls around it, and I am going to create a tremendous uproar in the country!"

The poor man said, "By the time you create the great uproar in the whole country and all the wells start having protecting walls, I will be dead. Just think of me first!"

The monk said, "Individuals don't matter, what matters is society." That is the Confucian idea. That is the idea of all socialists—that the individual does not matter.

The reason for China becoming communist is Confucius. For twenty-five centuries Confucius had been held in tremendous respect, so when Karl Marx became available to the Chinese, it fitted very well with the Confucian idea: the individual does not matter, what matters is the society.

The Confucian monk said to the man, "Anyway, any day you are going to die, so why not now? I cannot waste my time! I am going to create the revolution that will bring walls to every well in the whole country. Think of your children!" And the man went away.

The man in the well thought, "Strange ... I am dying here, and that idiot is going to create a revolution!"

A Buddhist monk passed by. He looked in the well. The man said, "Buddha has taught compassion. You should save me, I am dying! And it is getting darker and colder."

The Buddhist monk said, "Be patient. It is because of your past lives' evil acts that you have fallen into the well. Millions of people are here, and nobody else has fallen into the well. You must have committed very evil acts—murder, rape. It is better to clear the account.

"And Buddha has also said, 'Never interfere in anybody's life!' Just forgive me, I cannot interfere in your life. If I pull you out, you will fall in again because your punishment for the evil acts of the past life is not complete—so what is the point? Just die and be reborn, fresh, without any past evil acts hanging around you."

The man was so amazed, "These people are religious people?" And the Buddhist monk went away.

This is the logical consequence of Buddha, Mahavira, Krishna. All the Indian philosophies teach it. One of the Jaina sects, Terapanth, whose head is Acharya Tulsi, has seventeen hundred monks and three times more nuns. It is one of the strongest sects; very rich, super-rich people belong to it. The original man who created Terapanth sect, separate from mainstream Jainism, held the basic idea that if somebody is drowning, you should not interfere. That is the logical consequence of believing in past lives and evil acts and their punishment. If somebody is hungry, you should not interfere. If somebody is thirsty, you should not even tell him the way to the river. And, moreover, interfering in nature's course will create bad karmas for you. For example, if you pull a man out from the well, and tomorrow he commits a murder, do you think you are also responsible for it or not?

Logically, it seems to be perfectly right. If you had not saved the man, he would not have committed the murder. You are fifty percent responsible: you saved him, and he committed a murder. Now you will have to suffer for saving the man. Whatsoever he does from now onward, you will be responsible—for his whole life. You have unnecessarily disturbed his finishing of the punishment, and you have created, on the other hand, evil acts for which you will suffer in your future life.

So the Buddhist monk moved on from the well, and he was followed by a Christian missionary. The Christian missionary was carrying a bucket and a long rope. He immediately threw the rope and the bucket into the well, and pulled the man out.

The man said, "You are the only religious man."

The Christian missionary said, "In fact, I should be grateful to you, because unless you fall in the well I cannot earn virtue. I am against the Confucian idea that every well should have a wall. Then nobody will be falling in!—and for whom am I carrying the bucket and the rope? No walls are needed; otherwise, all virtue, all morality, all service will disappear from the world."

Bertrand Russell has made a very important statement: If there is no poverty, there will be no religion. Whom are you going to serve? If there is no death, all churches, all religions will become absolutely useless, invalid, out of date. They are surviving because of poverty, because of death, because of disease, because of orphans. That's why they are all against birth control—because birth control can destroy all poverty, and all the orphans can be stopped from coming into the world. What will happen to poor Mother Teresa? Who will give her a Nobel Prize? Orphans are absolutely needed, otherwise Mother Teresas will disappear. Poverty is needed, that's why they go on being against all birth control methods. It has nothing to do with God—they need the poor people, because their religion teaches them that if you serve the poor, if you open hospitals for the poor, if you open schools for the poor, you are earning a great bank balance in paradise.

This is not unselfishness. Who says it is unselfish? It is more selfish than anything else you can find in the world—a motivation to exploit poor people, people who have fallen into the well, people who are dying, people who are sick, people who are orphans. You are taking great advantage. All religions are exploiting your tremendous greed, in the name of virtue, in the name of unselfishness.

As a fundamental principal, I want you to remember that an unconscious person cannot act without motivation, and motivation is selfish, whatever you do.

I used to live in a city, teaching in the university, and a beautiful marble temple was being made there. For years I used to pass it on the road. Nine years I lived in that city, and the temple was just coming up, coming up, because they wanted to make something rare. Some super-rich man's father had died and it was his memorial. I had no idea about it, so one day I stopped my car and went inside where hundreds of marble workers were working. I asked the chief, "For what is this temple being raised?"

A man of great intelligence, he did not take me to the statue of Krishna which was placed in the middle of the temple. I was thinking he would take me to the statue, saying that the temple is being created for Krishna—but he took me behind the temple.

I said, "Where are you taking me?"

He said, "To the right place."

There was a big marble slab with the writing: "This temple is created by so-and-so in the memory of his great spiritual father."

He said, "For this stone the whole temple is being created. Krishna is just an excuse."

The unconscious mind cannot do anything without motivation. What will I get? And religions promise that in the future life, when he reaches to the pearly gates, Saint Peter will be standing there with all the angels singing "Alleluia!" and playing on their harps in your honor. It seems to be worthwhile to give something in charity, to do some virtuous act.

Unless an act is done without any motivation, it cannot be unselfish.

I want you to understand that except meditation there is no act that is unselfish, because it is only meditation which is going to dissolve your self, which is going to dissolve you into the whole. And once you are no more, whatever you do is going to be without motivation. Virtue comes out of a person who has become one with existence. Meditation is the door.

Meditation is the only unselfish act. But it appears that people who are engaged in meditation are just thinking of themselves, not bothering about the whole of humanity. Absolute nonsense! The people who are engaged in meditation are the only people who will find a place where there is no self, and all selfishness disappears. Then their whole life, their whole love, their whole compassion will be unmotivated. Whatever they do will be virtuous, because virtue can come only out of a conscious mind, an absolutely conscious mind.

In the conscious mind, totally conscious, there is not a single shadow of self. The totally conscious mind becomes qualitatively different from your unconscious mind. Hence it has been called no-mind, just to show the difference, otherwise you will get confused.

Mind is what you have. No-mind is the search of meditation. And from no-mind blossom flowers of unselfishness, of love, of compassion, of sharing.

I repeat Basho, the great Zen master, and one of the greatest poets of the world: "Sitting silently, doing nothing, the spring comes and the grass grows by itself." This sitting silently is not avoiding life. Sitting silently is searching for life, the very source of life. And the moment you have found the source, everything grows by itself, just like when spring comes, the grass grows by itself.

What is selfish in meditation? Just because you are sitting alone, closing your eyes, going inwards to find out the very source of your existence, is it selfish? By the time you find your authentic source of life, your self will have disappeared like a dewdrop in the early morning sun. You will come out without a self, just as a pure presence. Out of this pure presence radiates all that is virtuous.

Without meditation there is no virtue; there cannot be any virtue! And when I say anything like this, I say it with absolute authority, and I challenge every religion of the world to prove that unconscious people, sleepy people, can do any act without motivation. Selfishness means motivation, you are thinking of some reward.

An unselfish act means with no motivation, you are not thinking of any reward. You are doing it out of your abundance. You have too much, you are a rain cloud, you have to shower. And the more you share, the more starts coming to you. It is almost like a well of water: the more you draw the water, fresh water is coming into the well from all directions. But you become afraid that "If we take out the water, that much water is gone," it is better to keep the well closed.

It happened once ... Kahlil Gibran has a beautiful story.

In an ancient village there were two wells. One was in the palace, which was not available for anybody else than the royal family, and the other well was in the marketplace, which was available for everybody else except the royal family.

But one day a witch came into the town, and she chanted some gibberish and threw something inside the well. People watched but they could not understand what was happening. But by the time the sun was setting, everybody had drunk water from the well—except the royal family—and everybody had gone mad. The whole capital was mad, from the smallest child to the oldest man—except the king and the queen and the prince.

And a strange thing happened.... The whole crowd gathered around the palace and they started shouting that the king has gone mad. They were all mad, obviously, and they all agreed on the point that "The king does not seem to be the same as we are."

The king immediately asked his prime minister what to do. "Even our armies have gone mad. They are all dancing and they are asking, 'Come out of the palace! We will choose a new king who is sane just like us!'"

The prime minister was very old, an ancient wise man. He told the king, "The only way is to run from the back door. I will keep them engaged at the front door, telling them that 'I am bringing the king, he is getting ready.' You run to the well that they have been drinking the water from. Drink the water—you, your wife, your son—and you all get drunk. Unless you are mad this crowd is going to kill you!"

The advice was absolutely correct. The king and his family ran from the back door, drank quickly the water of the well that the witch had changed with a certain alchemical phenomenon. They did not come to the back door, they came dancing and rejoicing to the front gate, and the crowd was very happy that their king had become sane.

That night there was a great festival in the capital. "Our king, our queen, our future king—all have become sane!"

The crowd is living so unconsciously. You cannot expect from this crowd any act of virtue, any act of unselfishness. It is simply not possible. It is categorically impossible. First comes meditation, then everything else follows.

So when your parents or your priests tell you that you are doing a selfish act, tell them clearly that you are the only one who is going to drop the self, and there will be no selfishness left, and out of that state virtue will follow—"not from your prayers, not from your Bible or your Koran or your Gita, not from your teachings, but from my own exploration into whether there is a self."

The self is a shadow of unconsciousness, of darkness, of blindness. It has never been found by those who have entered deeper into themselves.

Nineteen

One Seed Can Make the Whole Earth Green

Osho,

What is compassion for a rebellious man?

Rebellion itself is the compassion. It is not a reactionary approach towards life. It is out of compassion that a man of understanding becomes a rebel. You are asking, "What is compassion for a rebellious man?" Rebellion itself is his compassion. It is out of compassion that he has become rebellious, otherwise there was no need for him.

What is the need for me to be a rebel? I could have lived silently in the Himalayas, without unnecessarily being bothered by all kinds of idiots. What am I going to gain by my rebelliousness and by my teachings about rebellion, except condemnation from all quarters, from all over the world? But there is no need for me to gain anything. What life could give to me it has given—it has given more than one could ask for. It is just out of love, out of compassion, that I will welcome any crucifixion, but I will continue till my last breath to raise people's consciousness, to instill their beings with the dreams of a beautiful future. And I will go on convincing them that the past has been ugly and nightmarish—that if you go on living according to the past, you don't have any more future.

It is not my personal problem. My past is finished. I don't have any future—I am not going to be reborn again. I could have remained completely indifferent to the problems of the world, to the problems of people; they are not my problems. I have struggled and come out of the jungle of all those problems. I am not going to be caught again in the net of a body. But with this enlightenment, this liberation, comes a tremendous compassion for all those who are struggling for the same aim. I would like that the world becomes more helpful to everybody to become awakened. Right now it is helpful only to keep you as asleep as possible.

Karl Marx was right when he said that religions have functioned like opium to the people. I may not agree with all his opinions, but about this small statement I agree one hundred percent. All the religions have been narcotics. They are the real drug dealers. They have kept humanity asleep, and they have taken away all the opportunities and possibilities of people becoming enlightened, of people becoming individuals, of people becoming free.

It is out of my love and compassion that I would like to go on sowing the seeds of rebellion in as many hearts as possible. Perhaps existence wants me to be a vehicle to save man from committing suicide—and not only to save man, but at the same time transform him also. Because this kind of man, as has existed in the past, is out of date, he cannot continue. Either he has to die or he has to transform.

Rebellion, to me, is the only saving device, and it is out of compassion—for no other reason.

> Hymie Goldberg was striding happily along the street on his way to work, when his old friend, Mr. Cohen, caught up with him.
>
> "You are pretty happy this morning," said Mr. Cohen.

"That's right," smiled Hymie, "I have finally cured my wife of her habit of yelling at me all the time."

"And how did you do that?" asked Mr. Cohen.

"Well," laughed Hymie, "I have convinced her that yelling at me was making a nervous wreck of the dog."

This is the situation of the present man. The wife is willing to stop yelling at poor Hymie Goldberg if she is convinced that her yelling will drive the dog insane. But if her yelling can drive the dog insane, what is it doing to poor Goldberg? That is not a consideration at all.

Man has lost compassion for man. He may be compassionate toward animals, he may be compassionate toward trees. In the Himalayas, there has been a movement going on for some years—a new concept. The people who live in the Himalayas love the trees and their trees are being cut, brutally, thousands every day. Just ten years ago an uneducated man started a movement, and it spread like wildfire all over the Himalayas. In the Himalayas, it is called "Chipko Andolan." It means, "cling to the tree movement." When people come to cut the tree, you simply cling, hug the tree, and be ready to die with the tree, but don't allow the tree to be cut.

So thousands of people are clinging to the trees, and the government contractors come and they are standing there... what to do? They cannot use their electric saws and cut the people with the trees. The movement is immensely successful, although the government is jailing, punishing those people who are preventing the trees from being cut. But the moment they are out of jail, they go back again. It seems they have slowed the process, and it is also possible that they may have succeeded.

These people—who are so compassionate to the trees that they are ready to die for them—murder human beings. With human beings their relationships are of cruelty, barbarousness. And they are primitive people; a few tribes even sacrifice men to their god, and then they eat the flesh of men. It is very strange that they are so compassionate toward the trees—to protect them they are ready to die; they risk imprisonment because they are preventing government work. But toward man they don't seem to have any compassion, any love. They beat their wives, they beat their children; they don't have any respect for their children, they don't have any respect for their women. In fact Hindu scriptures say that unless you beat your wife once in a while, you will lose control over her. It is absolutely according to religious scriptures, it is not a sin or a crime to beat your wife once in a while—that keeps peace in the house.

It would have been perfectly right if they had said that the wife is also allowed, once in while, to beat the husband; then it would have kept more peace in the house. If peace is the goal, then both should be given the opportunity to create it. And the people who have written such things are thought to be great saints! And if I say anything against them immediately somebody's religious feelings are hurt, immediately the government sends an arrest warrant. This has been going on my whole life.

Man has lost compassion completely—at least about other men. And I would like my people... their first duty is towards man, everything else comes next. If you are not loving and compassionate towards man, all your compassion for animals, dogs, is just stupid. One man in Mumbai has a trust... and we have been fighting a trust case for years. The government is not willing to accept this institution as a charitable trust, because to them teaching meditation is not charity. Teaching compassion is not charity, teaching charity is not charity. So I had told my people to look around and see what kind of charitable trusts are acceptable to the government. They found a trust in Mumbai that is tax-exempt, and the man who has that trust is a retired government officer; he collects donations for stray dogs.

Every day in his beautiful car he goes around the slums of Mumbai, where you will find stray dogs—and worse than that, stray human beings. Children with big bellies and shrunken bodies, standing by the side of the dogs just in the hope that they can get something to eat from the dog food. And that man, sitting in his car, is feeding the dogs; and those children are standing by the side waiting, so that if something is left they can eat it.

This is charity. And this man must be pocketing all the donations that are coming to him, because dogs cannot complain. They cannot say whether he comes every day or not, what kind of food is being given to them, whether it is edible or not, how much is being given, to how many dogs it is being given—dogs cannot report. It all depends on the man keeping the register to say that he is feeding five hundred dogs, or one thousand dogs, and how much money is being spent per dog.... And he goes on collecting donations, and the government allows him to be a tax-exempt, charitable trust.

This world certainly needs to be completely renewed. All old values have to be said goodbye to, and new values have to be established. This is possible only with a religious rebelliousness, not ordinary rebelliousness. Never before has a concept like religious or spiritual rebelliousness ever existed.

I am giving you a totally new philosophy, absolutely fresh. Political rebels have existed, but spiritual rebelliousness can only come out of compassion and meditation. And unless it comes out of meditation and compassion it is not worth anything. But I hope... in spite of the darkness all around, I still hope that when the darkness is too much, the dawn will be very close.

Twenty

I Belong to Eternity–You Can, Too

Osho,

Some people say that you are part of the New Age movement. I don't think so. Who is right, and what do you think about the New Age? Can it help people?

The New Age movement is just a fashion which will disappear very soon, as all your other movements have disappeared. Now you don't see hippies.... It is a very great phenomenon that so many hippies suddenly disappeared. What happened to their revolution? It was a revolutionary movement; it was dropping out of the society. Why have they dropped back into the society?

All these movements are very short-lived. They have beautiful names—that does not matter—but they don't have a radical philosophy to change human beings. The New Age movement has nothing unique which can transform individuals. It is a fashion; soon it will die—just a passing phase.

I am not part of any movement. What I am doing is something eternal. It has been going on since the first man appeared on the earth, and it will continue to the last man. It is not a movement, it is the very core of evolution.

So you are right that you don't count me as part of the new age movement. I am not. I am part of the eternal evolution of man. The search for truth is neither new nor old. The search for your own being has nothing to do with time. It is nontemporal.

I may be gone, but what I am doing is going to continue. Somebody else will be doing it. I was not here and somebody else was doing it. Nobody is a founder of it, nobody is a leader in it. It is such a vast phenomenon that many enlightened people have appeared, helped, and disappeared. But their help has brought humanity a little higher, made humanity a little better, a little more human. They have left the world a little more beautiful than they had found it.

It is a great contentment to leave the world a little better. More than that is asking too much. The world is too big; a single human individual is too small. If he can leave just a few touches to the painting, which for millions of years has been made by evolution, that's enough. Just a few touches... a little more perfection, a little more clarity.

I am not part of any fashion, any movement. I belong to eternity, and I would like you also to belong to eternity, not to a passing phase.

What do you say to the people who call you a utopian?

They are right—just their idea of utopia is not right. They think that utopia is something which cannot be achieved; that's exactly the meaning of the word *utopia*. Sir Thomas More wrote a book called *Utopia*, in which he hopes for everything that man has always aspired to but has never been able to achieve. There have been revolutions, there have been attempts to make alternative societies; all have failed. But that does not mean that we have made every possible effort.

I am reminded of Thomas Alva Edison. He was working on the electric bulb for three years continuously. All his colleagues were tired, bored, but they were puzzled and amazed that the old man would come to the lab before everybody else, full of zest, enthusiasm, hoping that it was going to happen today. Finally they said, "Three years we have been hearing about it; nine hundred experiments have been made—all have failed. But you seem to be absolutely unaffected by the failures."

Edison said, "No, I am not unaffected. I am immensely inspired. If nine hundred attempts have failed, it means now we are coming closer and closer every day to that attempt which is going to succeed. How long can it elude us? It is a challenge."

Do you see his point? He is saying nine hundred doors are closed. We have enquired: they are wrong doors, they lead nowhere. Now the number of doors is reduced. There are nine hundred doors less. We are succeeding; we are coming closer and closer to the door that will lead to the successful experiment.

Slowly, slowly his colleagues deserted him, his friends left him. But he continued, and one day he succeeded. It was late at night; it must have been three o'clock in the morning... the first light bulb! And he was so enchanted by it that he simply went on sitting under the light, looking at it. For five years he had been working.... And his wife shouted from the bedroom, "Are you mad or something? Put off that light and come to bed."

And he said to her, "You don't know what you are talking about. To put on this light I have wasted five years, lost all my friends and colleagues, and you are telling me to put it off? Just come and see the miracle."

I am a utopian. I am very optimistic. I trust in the inspirations, in the hopes of man. We have just been doing something wrong to materialize them. The basic thing that I want to point out to you is that we have always been thinking of changing the society. The communists, the fascists, the socialists, the Fabians, the anarchists, all kinds of utopians have one single thing in common, which is the cause of their failure. They all have tried to change the society.

The society does not exist anywhere.

What exists is the individual.

Society is only a name. Have you ever come across society? Have you ever met society and said hello... shaken hands with society? Whenever you come across anybody it is the individual.

The individual is the reality. Society is only a name.

They all tried to change the society, to change the individual. That was their wrong approach.

My effort is to change the individual.

The society will change by itself; it is simply a name. And to change the individual is not difficult, because each individual desires to be changed. No individual is satisfied as he is. He wants to be more conscious, to be more peaceful, to be more loving, to be more loved. He wants a life full of flowers and fragrance. What he finds is just misery, anxiety, anguish, meaninglessness.

What the individual is missing is a very simple thing: a certain methodology to make him more centered, more silent, more serene, more collected, more together. The name of the methodology is what I call meditation. The individual needs something more than the mind; it is already in him, but he is entangled with the mind. His entanglement with the mind prevents him from seeing beyond it to his real self.

Just a little effort for watching the mind, sitting silently, looking at the mind, as if it does not belong to you—and it does not belong to you...

You are the watcher; the mind is the watched.

You are the observer; the mind is the observed.

You are the subject; the mind is the object—you are not one.

Your subjectivity is your liberation—liberation from the mind. And once you are liberated from the mind, once you know that you are beyond the mind, miraculously a great mastery arises in you. The mind cannot pull you this way and that; it simply becomes a humble servant. The very presence of the master is enough for the mind to become an obedient servant. You can use it if you want. If you do not want to, you can say, "Shut up!" and you can remain in eternal peace and silence. The mind is a good mechanism, a biocomputer, but it is not the master.

This is the change that has to be spread to every individual on the earth, and then utopia is just around the corner of the road. Then it is not something which cannot be achieved. It can be achieved, and it should be achieved.

The people who have been calling me a utopian must be thinking that they are condemning me. They are wrong. I take it as a compliment! Give my thanks to them and tell them that I am a utopian, my people are utopians, and I want the whole world to become utopians.

OSHO INTERNATIONAL MEDITATION RESORT

The OSHO International Meditation Resort is a great place for holidays and a place where people can have a direct personal experience of a new way of living with more alertness, relaxation, and fun. Located about 100 miles southeast of Mumbai in Pune, India, the resort offers a variety of programs to thousands of people who visit each year from more than 100 countries around the world. Originally developed as a summer retreat for Maharajahs and wealthy British colonialists, Pune is now a thriving modern city that is home to a number of universities and high-tech industries. The Meditation Resort spreads over 40 acres in a tree-lined suburb known as Koregaon Park. The resort campus provides accomodation for a limited number of guests, in a new 'Guesthouse' and there is a plentiful variety of nearby hotels and private apartments available for stays of a few days up to several months.

Meditation Resort programs are all based in the Osho vision of a qualitatively new kind of human being who is able both to participate creatively in everyday life and to relax into silence and meditation. Most programs take place in modern, air-conditioned facilities and include a variety of individual sessions, courses and workshops covering everything from creative arts to holistic health treatments, personal transformation and therapy, esoteric sciences, the "Zen" approach to sports and recreation, relationship issues, and significant life transitions for men and women. Individual session and group workshops are offered throughout the year, alongside a full daily schedule of meditations. Outdoor cafes and restaurants within the resort grounds serve both traditional Indian fare and a choice of international dishes, all made with organically grown vegetables from the resort's own farm. The campus has its own private supply of safe, filtered water.
www.osho.com/resort

Some Other Titles From New Falcon Publications

Aleister Crowley's Illustrated Goetia
Taboo: Sex, Religion & Magick
Sex Magic, Tantra & Tarot: The Way of the Secret Lover
Enochian World of Aleister Crowley
    By Christopher S. Hyatt, Ph. D. and Lon Milo DuQuette

Cosmic Trigger 1
Cosmic Trigger 2
Cosmic Trigger 3
Coincidance
The Earth Will Shake
Email to the Universe
Nature's God
Prometheus Rising
TSOG: The Thing that Ate the Constitution
Wilhelm Reich in Hell
The Widow's Son
The Walls Came Tumbling Down
Sex, Drugs & Magick
Quantum Psychology
    By Robert Anton Wilson

Info Psychology
The Intelligence Agents
Neuropolitique
    By Timothy Leary, Ph. D.

The Eye in the Triangle
Healing Energy, Prayer and Relaxation
What you should know about the Golden Dawn
The Complete Golden Dawn System of Magic
The Golden Dawn Audio CD's
    By Israel Regardie

Zen without Zen Masters
    By Camden Benares

Aleister Crowley and the Treasure House of Images
    By J. F. C. Fuller, Aleister Crowley, David Cherubim,
    Lon Milo DuQuette and Nancy Wasserman

Please visit our website at http://www.newfalcon.com

New Falcon Publications
Publisher of Controversial Books and CDs
Invites You to Visit our Website:
http://www.newfalcon.com

At the Falcon website you can:

- Browse the online catalog of all our great titles including books by Robert Anton Wilson, Christopher S. Hyatt, Israel Regardie, Aleister Crowley, Timothy Leary, Osho, Lon Milo DuQuette and many more
- Find out what's available and what's out of stock
- Get special discounts
- Order our titles through our secure online server
- Find products not available anywhere else including:
    - One of a kind and limited availability products
    - Special packages
    - Special pricing
- And much, much more

Get online today at http://www.newfalcon.com